DO ANIMALS HAVE RIGHTS?

DO
ANIMALS
HAVE
RIGHTS?

ALISON HILLS

ICON BOOKS

Published in the UK in 2005
by Icon Books Ltd., The Old Dairy,
Brook Road, Thriplow,
Cambridge SG8 7RG
email: info@iconbooks.co.uk
www.iconbooks.co.uk

Sold in the UK, Europe, South Africa
and Asia by Faber and Faber Ltd.,
3 Queen Square, London WC1N 3AU
or their agents

Distributed in the UK, Europe, South Africa
and Asia by TBS Ltd., Frating Distribution Centre,
Colchester Road, Frating Green, Colchester CO7 7DW

Published in Australia in 2005
by Allen & Unwin Pty. Ltd.,
PO Box 8500, 83 Alexander Street,
Crows Nest, NSW 2065

Distributed in Canada by
Penguin Books Canada,
10 Alcorn Avenue, Suite 300,
Toronto, Ontario M4V 3B2

ISBN 1 84046 623 5

Typesetting by Hands Fotoset

Printed and bound in the UK by Cox and Wyman Ltd.

To Philip

ABOUT THE AUTHOR

Alison Hills studied philosophy at Cambridge University, becoming a Research Fellow of Clare College. She is now a Lecturer in Philosophy at the University of Bristol. She has written several articles about applied ethics and Kant's moral philosophy.

ACKNOWLEDGEMENTS

I would like to thank Tim Lewens, Rebecca Rushforth and Simon Flynn for their advice and encouragement; and in particular Paul Bou-Habib, Rowan Cruft, Finn Spicer and Marian Scott for their helpful comments on a previous draft of the book.

CONTENTS

LIST OF ILLUSTRATIONS

CHAPTER ONE

INTRODUCTION

In December 1998, the animal rights activist Barry Horne lay dying in prison. He had been found guilty of making a series of fire-bomb attacks that caused over £3 million worth of damage, and had been sentenced to eighteen years in jail. He was on his third hunger strike since his conviction and he intended to sacrifice his life to the cause of animal welfare.

At the same time, Robin Webb, spokesman of the Animal Liberation Front, read out a hit list of ten names issued by the Animal Rights Militia, an extremist animal rights organisation: if Horne died, the ten 'vivisectionists' would be assassinated. Among the ten was Colin Blakemore, Professor of Physiology at Oxford University, an expert in vision and the early development of the brain, whose research involved sewing shut the eyes of kittens. Not only did he experiment on animals himself, but he was also well known as a supporter of animal experimentation, arguing that it was essential to the progress of scientific and medical knowledge. Professor Blakemore was no stranger to threats from extremists: he had already been sent letter bombs and razors from animal rights activists.

Horne survived his hunger strike with his eyesight and his liver damaged. He died in 2001 after his fourth hunger strike, and was hailed as a martyr by animal rights organisations. Professor Blakemore continues his research in physiology, and supports scientific experiments on animals. He is still targeted by animal rights activists: often his house is surrounded by protestors and he cannot go out without a police escort.

Animal rights is an issue so emotive that some people are prepared to martyr themselves for the cause, and to threaten to kill other people for it. Yet many of us eat meat, wear leather and fur, and use medicines that have been tested on animals. People on each side of the debate have such strong passions and deeply held convictions that it is difficult for them to engage in a meaningful dialogue with their opponents. It is hard for a non-partisan to be sure what exactly are the arguments for and against granting rights to animals. Many of the books written about animal rights are extremist in one way or another: either they argue that animals and humans have equal rights; or they say that animals have no rights and that we may treat them in any way we want. But most of us don't accept either of these claims, but instead have a moderate view: we think that there are moral limits to what we may do to animals, but there are nevertheless important differences between humans and animals that warrant our treating them differently. This book defends the moderate view.

In early societies, people cared about their own family and perhaps their own tribe, but thought nothing of treating people from other tribes extremely badly. Today, however, most of us recognise that the people of our city, nation or race are of no greater value than those who live on the far side of the world. Many countries have signed up to the UN Declaration of Human Rights, acknowledging that all human life is of equal moral value and all of us have the same basic human rights.

However, many of us in the West believe that, though humans are all equally valuable, animals are not. We have been influenced greatly by the ancient Greek philosopher Aristotle and Christian writers such as Thomas Aquinas and St Augustine, all of whom claimed that humans are very different from other animals, and that we may use other animals, but not other humans, in any way that we please. But this Western tradition is thrown into doubt by Darwin's theory of evolution, and by our recognition that the view we have inherited from Aristotle and the early Christians is not the only way that we might conceive of the relationship between humans and animals. Buddhists, for example, have quite different views about animals and how we ought to treat them. Finally, modern philosophers like Peter Singer question the way we use non-human animals by asking whether we are guilty of prejudice against creatures that are not human. Our ordinary ways of thinking about animals and our everyday uses of them have been challenged. Can we defend them?

It is natural to think that some animals have minds that are very similar to ours: many animals can suffer pain and fear, some appear to be able to think, and some, like the great apes, can even be taught a basic language. But other animals seem to us very different: surely single-celled bacteria have no beliefs or feelings at all. But are the assumptions we make about animal minds justified? In the first part of this book, we look at the evidence that animals can suffer, have beliefs and reason as we do.

Many of us think that it is wrong to make other humans suffer for fun. It is wrong because we humans have moral status: it matters morally what happens to us. But do animals have this kind of moral status too? I argue that all sentient animals (that is, those that can feel pain and pleasure) have moral status: it matters morally when these animals suffer.

Having moral status is not the same as having rights, however. Some of our rights depend on our ability to think and to reason: a right to freedom of speech only makes sense for beings capable of communication. Many animal activists would not worry about denying animals the right to freedom of speech; however, their concern is with the most fundamental right of all, the right to life. They say that animals have a right not to be killed for food, for entertainment or for scientific research, just as humans do. Do humans alone have the right to life; or is it simple prejudice to deny animals that right too?

The final part of the book looks at the proper treatment of animals, given their moral status. Animals are a source of food for many of us: is it wrong for us to eat meat from animals that have been kept in the cramped unhealthy conditions of a factory farm? More fundamentally, is it morally acceptable to eat animals at all? We can eat well on a vegetarian diet; we do not *need* to eat meat in order to keep healthy. Most of us eat meat and fish for pleasure: is this morally wrong?

Many of us benefit from scientific research, using new medicines that were initially tested on animals. Scientists experiment on animals for many other reasons too: to test non-medical products like cosmetics and to find out more about human and animal biology. Are scientific experiments for any of these purposes morally legitimate?

The traditional British country pastime of hunting foxes, which has long been attacked by animal rights protestors, has recently been banned altogether in the UK. But what, if anything, is wrong with foxhunting? Is it the killing of the fox, or the way that it is killed in a hunt that is objectionable?

Each of these issues needs to be addressed separately, for it might be acceptable for us to use animals in some of these ways but not others: perhaps it is wrong to breed animals for food in factory farms, but not wrong to eat animals; it may be cruel to make animals suffer for our amusement, but permissible to injure them in medical experiments that greatly benefit us. We need to give due weight both to our rights and interests and to the moral status of animals. In deciding how we should treat animals, we have to reflect on fundamental issues about ourselves: on the value of human life and on what it is to be human.

CHAPTER TWO

ANIMAL RIGHTS
THROUGH THE AGES

The hare laughed when the tortoise took up his challenge of a race. Having moved into a commanding lead, he thought he would demonstrate his effortless superiority by taking a brief nap before finishing the contest. Meanwhile the determined tortoise, unfazed by these antics, plodded on, crossing the finish line just as the hare woke up, cursing. So we learn that flashy arrogance will get its come-uppance, while slow but steady wins the day.

The wolf inveigled his way into the middle of a flock of lambs by covering his own fur with a sheep's fleece, and made off with his dinner. The industrious ant warned the flighty grasshopper that leaner times were around the corner, but to no avail. The peacock asked Juno for a beautiful voice to accompany his splendid appearance, but had to learn to make do with what he had already got.

Children have been fascinated by Aesop's fables for thousands of years. In these stories, animals play two contrasting roles. They take on familiar human characteristics and teach us about ourselves: lions are powerful and proud but can be tyrannical; foxes and wolves are cunning, and will try to trick you with their silver tongue and deceptive appearance; ants are hardworking and thrive even in the hardest times. But at the same time these animals are not like us; there are no complex human characters, mixtures of good and bad, here. Nor are these talkative creatures accurate portraits of real animals; they are far too articulate and sophisticated.

In the ancient world, people lived side-by-side with animals, and were probably better placed to observe them than most of us are today. They felt the same tension, between seeing animals as just like us and as quite dissimilar, which is played out both in Aesop's fables and in the arguments of philosophers, then as well as now, about the way that animals ought to be treated.

Like us, the people of ancient Greece and Rome ate animals, hunted them, admired and loved them. They farmed the same kinds of animal that we do: cattle, pigs, sheep and goats. In their small farms, the livestock would roam outside in fields; many people kept a few chickens or a goat themselves. Most ordinary people usually could not afford meat, instead eating mostly vegetables; beef was a rare treat.

In pre-industrial societies like those of the ancient world, animals were also valued for their work: oxen pulled carts and ploughs; dogs were used to guard sheep and houses; men and animals worked together on the farm.

Just as horse-racing and bull-fights are watched by millions today, in the ancient world, animals were involved in many kinds of entertainment. Sometimes, as in the popular chariot-racing, no animals were injured, but often spectators were amused simply by watching animals die. In amphitheatres throughout the Roman world, leopards, lions, tigers, bears and elephants would be encouraged to fight, either against one another or matched with men, from professional huntsmen to unarmed victims. Bloodthirsty crowds appreciated the skills of the hunters but were impressed by the staggering slaughter: hundreds of animals would be killed in each show.

Whereas using animals for food, work and entertainment is familiar to us today, one significant role of animals in the ancient world is almost entirely foreign: the religious sacrifice.

It is hard to overstate the importance of animal sacrifice in the religions of ancient Greece and Rome. By ritually killing an animal, any ordinary person could thank the gods, ask a favour or find out what they willed. Myths telling of the pleasure taken by the gods in human sacrifice were common in Greek culture; animals were sacrificed as a substitute. Either the animal would be burnt whole with wine and incense, sometimes with a few drops of human blood symbolically added; or parts of the animal would be burnt and the rest eaten. The larger the number of animals, the more pleasing to the gods: a sacrifice of a hundred bulls was not unusual. The killing of animals was so fundamental that it was nearly impossible to oppose it without challenging traditional religion altogether.

What did ancient philosophers think about the slaughter of hundreds of animals for entertainment, or their ritual sacrifice in religious ceremonies? The most influential ancient writer on animals was the Greek philosopher Aristotle (384–322 BC).

Aristotle had quite a low opinion of the intellect of animals. It was common among the Greeks to link reason with speech (the same word, *logos*, could be used for both), as if thinking were like talking quietly to oneself. Though aware that animals could make noises – grunts and howls – Aristotle insisted that they could not speak a proper language and concluded that they had no beliefs at all. He was also convinced that no animal was capable of true loyalty, courage or any other virtue, as no animal could understand the difference between right and wrong. Animals have nothing in common with us, he said, and so in terms of justice, we owe them nothing: we may treat them as we like.

Some ancient Greeks disagreed with Aristotle; whereas Aristotle claimed that we had nothing in common with animals, Pythagoras (c. 580–c. 500 BC) believed that humans and animals were both made of the same elements: that the breath that gave life to us also gave life to animals, and that animals could be reincarnated as humans. He and his followers opposed cruelty to animals as well as animal sacrifice.

Theophrastus (c. 372–287 BC), a student of Aristotle, also rejected his views about animals. He argued that it was wrong to kill animals and make them suffer, because animals were just like us: their bodies had the same kind of fluids and tissues as ours; they had emotions and feelings and were capable of some kinds of reasoning too.

There were considerable differences of opinion about

animals in the ancient world: some philosophers argued that killing animals was wrong. But the popular morality of the time saw nothing objectionable in eating animals, sacrificing them to the gods, or watching them die in the amphitheatre. Aristotle too denied that we owed anything to animals and it was he, not his critics, who had the most lasting influence on Western culture.

God's Creatures

Christianity arose in the ancient world, and immediately distinguished itself from ancient Greek and Roman religions by opposing animal sacrifice. But early Christians like St Paul did not base their objections on concerns about animal welfare. St Paul believed that Christ's supreme sacrifice made all such practices obsolete: in his eyes, sacrifices of animals were pointless, rather than cruel. Despite rejecting animal sacrifice, Christians generally emphasised the difference between humans and other animals: we are made in the image of God, only a little lower than the angels; animals are another thing entirely.

The major Christian thinkers, St Augustine (354–430 AD) and Thomas Aquinas (c. 1225–74), argued that animals are not within our moral community because they have no reason. Both were influenced greatly by Aristotle, so important in the Middle Ages that he was known simply as 'The Philosopher'. Both appealed to the Bible's claim that humans have 'dominion' over the other animals (Genesis 1:26–30), interpreting this as meaning that humans were entitled to use animals as they saw fit, even if that included killing them or causing them to suffer (though according to later chapters of Genesis, the 'dominion' of man over the other animals may not include eating them, for Adam and Eve were vegetarian in the Garden of Eden).

Aquinas thought that the great divide between humans and animals lay in the fact that humans alone had an immortal soul. This view has three important implications. First, all humans are valuable in virtue of our immortal soul. And, since each of us, no matter how young or old, rich or poor, beautiful or ugly, clever or stupid, has a soul, we are all equally valuable. Second, the decision of whether we should live or die belongs to God, not to us, so we have no right to kill anyone who has a soul. All human life is sacred; we all have a right to life, but animals, without an immortal soul, do not. Third, since we are much more valuable than soul-less animals, we have dominion over them and are entitled to use them for our own purposes.

The Christian view of the essential equality of all man-kind is totally different from the ancient Greek and Roman conception of humanity. Aristotle thought that noble and virtuous men deserved more than the weak and corrupt: it was obvious to him that men were not all equally valuable. But the Aristotelian and Christian views of animals were similar: animals were a lower kind of creature, quite differ-ent from man, which we might use in any way we pleased. Although some Christians, including the followers of St Francis, emphasised the importance of treating animals well, in recognition of their value as part of God's creation, the idea of man having dominion over the animals was much more dominant in Christian thought, and still influences the way we think of animals and the way we treat them today.

The Descent of Man

According to Christianity, we humans are 'higher beings' only a little lower than the angels; we have dominion over all other animals, which have no soul. But the biologist Charles Darwin (1809–82), investigating the origin of species, explained how closely we are related to other animals and called into question the Christian image of man as a being of quite a different kind from them.

Christianity taught that God created all non-human animals in one single day; Aristotle believed that the same kinds of animals had always existed. Darwin showed that both these claims are wrong: all the different species that exist today have evolved from common ancestors. In each generation, animals mate and have a number of offspring that are copies of their parents, each with slight changes. These animals are very similar to one another, but some, for example, can run a little faster or have better eyesight or hearing, which means they can survive better in their environment and can produce more offspring. So the 'fittest' creatures thrive and their numbers increase. Groups of similar animals evolve in different ways, often because they are in diverse environments, one group living in a forest, another by a lake, for example. The groups of animals eventually become so different from one another that they can no longer mate successfully: they are then classed as belonging to different species.

Darwin called this process 'evolution by natural selection' and he did not restrict its application to non-human animals. He showed that biologically, there is no great divide between humans and non-human animals. We are particularly closely related to chimpanzees, with whom we now know that we share over 98 per cent of our DNA.

Do Darwin's ideas have implications for our treatment of animals? His theory forces us to rethink our relationship with other animals. If we should have 'dominion' over them, it is not because we are higher beings of a different origin from them; we have the same ancestors as other animals. Nor can it be because we are very different from other animals in our biology or physiology. The theory of evolution does not rule out the possibility that there is some other reason why we have dominion over the animals, even though our biology is similar to theirs and we have evolved from the same stock. But it is also compatible with Darwin's theory that we are not superior to other animals, that we should try to treat them well, perhaps even as well as we treat other humans.

Darwin himself was deeply concerned by cruelty to animals, but he also cared about the progress of science. He campaigned on behalf of animal experimentation, believing that increasing our understanding of physiology would benefit mankind. Though he acknowledged that we ought not to treat animals in any way that pleases us, he believed that we are entitled to use animals if we will substantially benefit from doing so.

Animals as Property

Darwin's view that unnecessary cruelty to animals is wrong, but that some uses of animals are legitimate, is similar to the conception of the proper treatment of animals enshrined in the laws of many countries today. In the UK, for example, there are laws against animal cruelty, but killing animals for food and experimenting on them is permitted.

In Britain before 1822, the law viewed animals merely as property, as things to be protected not for their own sake, but for the sake of their owner. If I own a table, it is against the law for you to steal it or destroy it, and if you do steal it or attack it with an axe, you should be punished. But it is obvious that the law protects the table, not because it is worth protecting for its own sake, but for my sake, so that I can continue to enjoy using it, because there are no laws governing my treatment of my own table. If I want to hack it to pieces myself, or sell it to someone who will chop it up, the law will not condemn me or punish me.

Laws treating animals as property protected those animals from being stolen ('poached') or attacked by people who did not own them, punishing the poaching of deer, fish and cattle by death. But there were no laws governing the treatment of those creatures by their owners. Just as I could do what I liked to my own table, I could do what I liked to my own livestock. If my animal attacked someone else, I could be held accountable, and the law might intervene if I hit my horse in the street and a crowd gathered to watch, causing a public disturbance. But according to the law, there was nothing wrong with my beating my own horse in the privacy of my own home.

When animals are viewed as mere property, the legal presumption is that whatever you do to animals that you own or that are not owned by anyone is acceptable unless there is a specific law against it. There is an assumption that people who experiment on animals, hunt them or kill them for food have a *right* to do so. If you change the law to ban some of those practices, it looks like you are unfairly restricting human rights, especially people's rights over their own property. Early animal welfare campaigners found it very difficult to get the law on animals changed.

In the early 1800s, attempts were made in the UK to ban popular entertainments like bear-baiting, which involved tying a bear to a stake and encouraging several vicious dogs to attack it. There were two grounds for banning such pastimes: they were cruel and they caused public disorder (many criminals gathered together to watch the show). These attempts at bans failed, but in 1822, the first animal welfare law in Britain was passed: it became an offence for anyone to treat 'wantonly and cruelly' any cattle, sheep or horse, on pain of a fine. In 1835 the act was extended to cover dogs and other domestic animals (and imprisonment was introduced as a possible punishment); animal fighting and baiting were prohibited. At about the same time, some other countries also passed animal cruelty laws. For

William Hogarth, *Cockpit*. These entertainments were banned by some of the earliest animal welfare legislation

example, in the USA, laws were passed banning the unjustified infliction of pain on animals; but they did not have much impact, as almost any human use of animals was considered legitimate, no matter how the animals suffered, on the basis that man had dominion over the animal world.

Since 1835, UK law has usually regulated activities rather than banned them outright. For example, in 1876 the Cruelty to Animals Act was passed to regulate animal experimentation: it became an offence to perform an experiment giving pain to a living animal, unless that experiment would advance physiological knowledge, reduce suffering or prolong life. Currently in the UK, scientists must have a licence to experiment on animals, and their project must also have a licence; animal experiments are permitted only if they are expected to give us significant benefits and there are no adequate alternatives. There is, however, no international consensus on laws governing animal experimentation. The UK laws are currently among the most demanding in the world. In the USA, whose scientists carry out more experiments on animals than those of any other country, there are some protections for animals. Some South American countries have no legislation at all.

There are also laws regulating farming, a practice that has changed enormously since the first British animal welfare laws in 1822. Many of us like to picture farms in which animals roam freely across wide-open fields, fed and tended by a jolly farmer who knows each cow by name and looks after each newborn lamb like one of his own children. Of course, no farm was ever quite like this ideal, but today many are 'factory farms', on an enormously large scale, ruthlessly commercial and prepared to impose any amount of suffering on farm animals if doing so will increase profits. In factory farms, chickens are kept in tiny cages that prevent them stretching their wings or turning round, in windowless sheds with no natural light that house up to 100,000 birds. As so many birds live so close together, diseases are common: one of the main jobs for the 'farmer' is to remove the bodies of dead birds.

In the UK, the USA and many other countries, the laws applying to factory farms permit chickens to be kept in very small cages, though some European countries including Switzerland are committed to phasing out battery farming. The rules for cows, pigs and sheep are typically more strict. But the legal regulation of factory farms has more than one purpose: as well as preventing cruelty to animals and improving animal and human health, it also protects the commercial interests of the factory farm. The resulting laws have strange anomalies: according to British law you, an ordinary person, might be prosecuted for keeping a chicken in a pen the size of an A4 piece of paper but factory farmers would not, as it is considered too costly for them to provide larger cages.

Much of our 'common-sense' attitude towards animals in modern Western countries is influenced by Aristotle's view that we owe nothing to animals because they have nothing in common with us, and the Judaeo-Christian view that man has dominion over the other animals. We treat animals as our property; we kill and eat them and experiment on them when we want to. We have some laws preventing animal cruelty, but make sure that they are not so strict that they interfere with our eating meat as cheaply as possible. But what seems obvious to us is quite alien to societies influenced by other ethical and religious traditions, which view animals rather differently.

The Wheel of Life

Buddhists divide the world into two categories: the physical universe, and the life-forms (*sattva*) which live in it. The physical universe forms world-systems which undergo cycles of evolution and decline over billions of years. *Dharma* is the universal law that governs the physical and moral order of the universe; Buddhists picture the physical and moral worlds as intertwined. If the farmers become more lazy the land may become more barren: a decline in morals can lead to physical deterioration.

Within a world-system there are various realms of rebirth: gods, humans, titans, ghosts, animals, hell, all depicted in the 'wheel of life' (*bhavacakra*). Hell is the worst place to be, a place of torment. Rebirth as an animal is better than hell, but not a great deal better: animals are governed by brute instinct, and lack the intellectual capacity to understand their situation or to improve it. Next is the realm of ghosts, former humans who have strong desires that they can never satisfy binding them to the earth. Above the ghosts are the 'titans', who are violent and desire power; and then the human realm, a desirable realm that is difficult to attain. Humans have reason and free will, and can use these to understand the *dharma* and implement Buddhist teachings. At the highest levels are the gods. You can move up or down these realms depending on how well you live your life, through *karma*, a kind of natural law.

Both animals and humans, unlike the higher gods, are in

the sphere of 'sense-desires', but we humans are the higher life-form, with a greater capacity for moral and spiritual development. Nevertheless, we do not have dominion over the animals: we should be kind to lesser beings, rather than exploiting them. A human who treated animals particularly badly might well return, through *karma*, as an animal. Buddhists believe that we should try to avoid inflicting suffering on animals as well as on humans: we should show compassion for every sentient creature.

Buddhists also believe in *ahimsa* or the inviolability of life. They reject animal sacrifice (which had been common in early Indian religion), they do not usually permit harming or killing animals in scientific experimentation, and they do not think that anyone should kill an animal for food. There are, however, some misconceptions in the West about the traditional Buddhist attitude towards vegetarianism. Traditional Buddhists reject the killing of animals, including the killing of animals for food, but not the eating of animal flesh. If the animal is already dead – and it has not been killed on your behalf – its meat is 'blameless' and you are permitted to eat it. Even a Buddhist monk, even the Buddha himself, would eat meat that is 'pure' in this way. There are restrictions on what meat monks may eat, but these prohibitions tend to be symbolic: they may not eat elephants or horses, symbols of royalty; dogs and snakes, which are considered disgusting; and lions, tigers, bears and hyenas, for it is too dangerous to try to kill them.

Unlike the Aristotelian–Christian tradition, Buddhism emphasises the similarity between humans and animals, as creatures that can feel and suffer, and claims that we owe to animals duties similar to the duties we owe to humans.

Animal Liberation

The modern animal welfare movement was galvanised by the publication of *Animal Liberation*, often known as the 'animal rights bible', written by the philosopher Peter Singer in 1975. The book is about 'the tyranny of humans over non-human animals'; it is a political work whose aim is to force us to question our treatment of animals and our attitudes towards them. Singer reports in considerable detail many examples of the deeply unpleasant ways animals are used in scientific experiments and in factory farming; his book has been very effective in changing many people's views about animals and converting them to vegetarianism.

Singer is a utilitarian. Utilitarians believe that it is our moral duty to bring about as much happiness and as little suffering as possible; they think it is wrong to steal and to kill because stealing and killing tend to lead to more suffering than happiness.

Suppose that I am wondering whether to give some money to charity or to buy myself a couple of new CDs. As a utilitarian, I should try to work out how much pleasure I would gain by buying myself the CDs: quite a bit, if they are any good! Then I should work out how much suffering I would relieve by giving the money to charity. By making a donation to charity, I could save the lives of some children who live in great poverty on the other side of the world.

Even though these children are strangers to me and I may never meet them in the rest of my life, their suffering and pleasure count equally with mine. Even if I would enjoy my new CDs a lot, these children will benefit more from my money; so, according to utilitarianism, I should send the money to charity.

Utilitarians think that pleasure and pain, happiness and suffering are morally important, no matter who rejoices or suffers, whether it is I or distant children I never meet. It does not even matter whether it is other humans who are affected. If cats and dogs, pigs and sheep can feel pain and pleasure, they count too, as the utilitarian Jeremy Bentham (1748–1832) wrote:

> The question is not, Can they *reason*: nor, Can they *talk*, but Can they *suffer*?

According to utilitarianism, all sentient creatures have an equal moral status: their pain and pleasure should count equally when we decide what to do.

Animals kept in factory farms suffer terribly. They live in uncomfortably small pens, are fed inappropriate foods to fatten them as quickly as possible, and suffer from disease because so many are kept close together. Of course, many humans benefit from factory farming: the farmers themselves make large profits, and many people enjoy eating the cheap meat the farming produces. But Singer argues that the suffering of factory-farmed animals far outweighs these human pleasures: factory farming is wrong; we should stop supporting these farms and stop eating factory-farmed meat. In fact, any large-scale farming of animals is likely to lead to more suffering than pleasure, he claims, so it would be best if we became vegetarians and stopped eating animals altogether.

Singer argues for other changes in our attitudes to animals too. He thinks that the benefits of scientific experimentation on animals do not outweigh the suffering imposed on those animals: most experiments on animals are morally wrong and should be banned.

Of course, Singer is very much aware that most of us do not count the suffering of animals equally with our own suffering and pleasure; we act as if our pleasure in eating meat is far more important than the suffering of factory-farmed animals. But he thinks our attitude is simply a mistake: it is an example of 'speciesism'. Just as racism is a prejudice in favour of your own race, speciesism is a prejudice in favour of your own species: humans are speciesist whenever they favour humans over other animals. Singer thinks that we are guilty of speciesism whenever we allow an animal to be treated in ways that we would never permit of a human child of similar mental capacity. We would never kill a human child for food, however brain-damaged, so why do we think that such treatment is acceptable for a sensitive and intelligent animal like a pig?

Singer is a powerful advocate for the better treatment of animals, and is certainly an important influence on the recent changes in the law that have given more emphasis to animal welfare. But he is not a supporter of animal rights. According to utilitarianism, if killing an animal, or even a human, would bring about more happiness than anything else, we ought to commit murder. Of course, it is very unusual for murder to lead to happiness rather than misery, so for the most part utilitarians will not support it. But in exceptional circumstances, for the utilitarian, murder is the right thing to do; since no one has the right not to be killed in those circumstances, no one has a right to life. Many people find this implication of utilitarianism troubling. This is a problem for Singer, because his defence of animal welfare is based on his utilitarianism, and if we question that theory, we must also question his conclusions about how we ought to treat animals.

Even if we reject his utilitarian theory, however, Singer gives us a difficult problem to consider. Many of us treat animals very differently from how we treat humans. We eat animals, we allow them to be killed for our benefit in scientific experimentation. But when we are asked *why* it is wrong to kill humans for food, but fine to kill animals, we do not know what to say. Surely the fact that an animal is not of our own species cannot be so very important?

Singer presents us with a dilemma. Either we must point to the difference between animals and humans that explains why we are entitled to eat animals and experiment on them, even though it is wrong to do the same to humans. Or we must accept that it is *not* true that animals have 'nothing in common with us', and we must treat them with as much consideration as we give to other humans. Anyone, whatever they think about utilitarianism, must answer Singer's dilemma.

PART ONE

ANIMAL MINDS

CHAPTER THREE

CAN THEY SUFFER?

It was spring, and a mole was working hard in his burrow. But this was no ordinary mole, and no ordinary work: he brushed and dusted and painted his home with whitewash until he felt so frustrated that with a heartfelt 'Hang spring-cleaning', he ran away to the riverbank.

Thus begins Kenneth Grahame's novel *The Wind in the Willows*, in whose pages we are introduced to the timid Mole, good-hearted Ratty, grumpy Badger and conceited Toad, who go on adventures, enjoy picnics of potted meat with pickled gherkins and ginger beer, love rowing little boats and driving motorcars and, all in all, act exactly like good English gentlemen of the Edwardian era.

This charmingly outrageous anthropomorphism is not to be taken seriously – we are not likely to mistake these characters for real creatures: we know that animals do not wear slippers or sit in armchairs. But some philosophers and scientists believe that we are nevertheless prone to more insidious forms of confusion. Though we may feel confident that some animals have thoughts and feelings as we do, where, they ask, is the scientific evidence confirming that we are right?

Mole and Ratty discuss the meaning of life © E.H. Shepard 1933, reproduced by permission of Curtis Brown Ltd., London

It may seem obvious that your cat Felix feels pain when you pull her tail, or that your dog Rover would suffer if you kicked him. But it is not so obvious that all animals can feel pain: what about fish, mussels, slugs or ants? How can we tell whether worms feel anything at all?

The question of whether animals can feel pain is part of a wider problem of whether animals are conscious. Do they have an inner mental life? We see things as coloured, as bright or dark; we hear and taste things; we have pleasant and painful experiences. We assume that Felix and Rover have experiences too, perhaps rather different from ours because their ways of sensing the world are not like ours, but we think that *there is something it is like* to be Felix or

Rover, just as there is something it is like to be you or me. We are less confident that there is something it is like to be an ant, slug or bacterium. But are we right to be so sure that Felix and Rover have an internal life? Perhaps we humans are the only ones to have any experiences at all. If only humans were conscious, then only we could suffer, and we would have no need to worry about causing animals pain.

Even if we are convinced that animals are conscious, there is a second very important question: what kinds of experiences are they having? If we care about animal suffering, we have to have some way of telling when they are having painful experiences and how unpleasant those experiences are. But we can be pretty sure that the inner life of some creatures is quite different from ours. Bats experience the world through their hearing: they make high-pitched noises and work out where objects around them are placed by the echoes of those sounds. We can try to imagine what it would be like to be a bat, but it is extremely difficult for us to know what it is really like: do bats get a picture of the world through echo-location as we do through our eyes, or is it quite different? It is hard for us to know which experiences are unpleasant for animals and how unpleasant they are. I can imagine what it would be like for *me* to be caged like a lion in a zoo; but I have really no idea whether what the *lion* experiences is at all similar. So even if we were convinced that animals could suffer, we would need to know a lot about their inner experiences if we wanted to avoid causing them suffering.

Perhaps we ought not to worry about what kind of experiences animals have, however, until we are confident that they have an inner mental life at all.

Living Robots

René Descartes (1596–1650) thought that animals were like robots, without minds and unable to feel pain. By contrast, he believed that humans had a soul, in virtue of which we can think, have desires, hopes, dreams and feelings. Our minds reside in our souls, which are separate from our bodies: our souls can live on after our bodies die. But the mental and the physical can interact: if you drop a heavy rock on to your toe, the physical world (rock hitting toe) will cause a change in your mind (your toe will hurt), and that may in turn change the physical world (you will shout 'ow' and start to limp). Descartes thought that the soul and the body interacted in a special part of the brain, called the pineal gland.

Descartes' view that our minds and bodies are separate is known as Cartesian dualism. This theory does not rule out the possibility that animals have minds: because minds are quite separate from the physical world, many kinds of animal with very different brains and nervous systems from ours might have a soul and therefore a mind. But since animals cannot talk or reason, Descartes thought that they in fact had no soul. He admitted that animals sometimes act in ways that make us imagine that they feel pain. If a heavy rock drops onto the foot of your dog, Rover, he will make noises and limp too. But this does not prove that he is suffering, for his brain may cause him to act that way when a rock drops on his foot, even though he feels nothing at all.

Scientists who followed Descartes put these ideas into practice, as an unknown contemporary of Descartes described:

> They administered beatings to dogs with perfect in-difference and made fun of those who pitied the creatures as if they felt pain. They said the animals were clocks; that the cries they emitted when struck were only the noise of a little spring that had been touched, but that the whole body was without feeling.

It is tempting to think that the scientists who followed Descartes adopted his views as an excuse for carrying out their gruesome experiments without guilt. It may be *convenient* for us to claim that animals do not feel pain, but surely we know that their suffering is real.

But we cannot just dismiss Descartes' view. We say that the beaten dogs cried *because* they were in pain; we explain their actions in terms of what they thought and felt. According to Descartes, we should explain the dogs' cries mechanistically. A clock chimes on the hour because inside it are various parts arranged appropriately. It is absurd to think that the clock wants to chime, or feels like chiming, that it chimes because it is happy, or to attract attention when it is feeling miserable. The clock doesn't feel a thing. Perhaps the parts of the dog are arranged so that it barks automatically when it is hit; but it suffers no more than a chiming clock.

Descartes explains animal behaviour as similar to the way that we humans respond when our reflexes are triggered. If you are hit just below your knee, your leg will jump upwards. You respond to being hit; but you don't feel any pain. Similarly, animals may respond to an injury by moving away and crying out, without feeling anything.

We now have two alternative accounts of what happens to dogs when they are beaten: which should we prefer? It is generally accepted that when we choose between two theories, we should use 'Ockham's Razor': we should prefer the theory that explains the phenomenon in the simplest way. The best theory would explain everything we wanted in as simple terms as possible. Descartes' explanation is simpler than ours. We have to assume that animals can feel pain, *as well as* that their bodies are organised so that they respond when hurt. Descartes just has to assume that their bodies are arranged to respond when injured: he can explain the same behaviour while making fewer assumptions. In that respect, his mechanistic explanation is better than ours, but only if it can adequately explain all animal behaviour.

Behaviourism: 'Scientific' Psychology

In the early 20th century, psychologists were worried that studies of animals were unscientific. Some animal researchers were lapsing into talk of the feelings and beliefs of animals, talk which these psychologists considered to be anthropomorphic nonsense. They insisted that psychologists should describe both their experiments and the animals' behaviour in neutral, physical terms. For example, a researcher might be interested in what happens to rats when they are repeatedly given electric shocks. A *scientific* psychologist would describe the experiment in physical terms – the rat was given a certain number of electric shocks of a certain intensity – and describe the animal's response in physical terms: the rat made a number of noises and sustained injuries of a particular kind. To say that the rat acted as if it were in agony would be inappropriately going beyond a pure science.

This 'behaviourism' was advocated by John Watson (1878–1958) and B.F. Skinner (1904–90). According to Skinner, animal behaviour did not depend on genetics at all, but could be explained entirely through the animal's inter-action with its environment. A rat can learn to act in a certain way – for example, to press a lever – by 'positive reinforcement': if the rat is rewarded with food for pressing the lever, it will learn to keep pressing it. Behaviourists mostly experimented on rats and pigeons, but believing that environment alone affected behaviour, they thought there were no significant differences between different species of animal: what they found out through experiments on rats could in principle be applied to any other animal. Skinner and Watson did not treat humans differently from other animals; in their view, humans too learnt through positive reinforcement, and a scientific human psychology would not mention mental states at all.

According to Skinner and Watson, the proper methodology for psychology was to use only physical descriptions of behaviour. They were *methodological behaviourists*. Some philosophers, like Ludwig Wittgenstein (1889–1951), went further, arguing that the very idea of inner experiences does not make sense. When I use the word 'pain', I can't be talking about an inner experience, he claimed. For if I were, since I can never know for sure whether anyone else feels the way I do, I could never know whether they were using the word 'pain' in the same way as I was or whether we were constantly talking at cross-purposes. And further, no one could have taught me to use the word in the first place. Though a word like 'pain' seems to be used of inner mental states, really it must concern observable outward behaviour. This philosophical theory about the meaning of words like 'pain' is called *logical behaviourism*.

According to both kinds of behaviourists, a true scientist would not use any mental terms. But it proved very difficult if not impossible for researchers to describe animal behaviour without referring to feelings. There is a huge variety of behaviour associated with feeling pain: cringing, crying out, limping, avoiding the source of the pain, cradling the part of the body that has been hurt and so on. It is nearly impossible to describe all of these accurately in purely physical terms, but it is very straightforward if you are permitted to say: the rat acted as if it were in pain.

Behaviourists have particular problems when mental states interact with one another, because the creature will act quite differently from how it would if it had either mental state without the other. If you are in pain, but you don't want anyone else to know that you are, you will try not to cry out or limp. Similarly, if a rabbit has hurt its leg, but does not want a fox to know that it is weak and cannot run, it will try not to limp. How can a behaviourist explain a rabbit trying to disguise its limp without mentioning its pain, its beliefs and its desires?

Behaviourists were right to emphasise the links between different types of mental states, their causes, and the kind of behaviours that express them: pain is often caused by an injury, and is expressed by crying out and moving away from the source of the injury. But they were completely wrong to say that it is unscientific to think that animals and humans have minds. We cannot understand humans or animals properly without making sense of their inner mental states, so we have to reject theories like behaviourism that deny that humans and animals have minds.

Evidence for Pain

Imagine that you burn yourself on a hot frying pan, twist your knee stepping in a rabbit hole, fall ill with influenza, or hit your head on a low door-frame. Obviously you will be in pain. How do you know that you're in pain? That's obvious too: you can feel it! Each of us knows in a very direct way when we are in pain. But we cannot be so sure about other people.

If you see me touch a hot frying pan, how do you know what I am feeling? You know that in the same circumstances, your hand would be hurting; you can imagine what it would feel like if you touched the pan. You see me reacting in the same ways that you would if you were in pain: I drop the pan, clutch my hand and cry out. Perhaps I even tell you how much it hurts, and beg you to do something about it.

You may have some scientific knowledge about human physiology: you know that all humans have similar nervous systems. Since your own nervous system causes you to feel pain when you touch a hot frying pan, it is likely that mine does the same for me.

Of course, some people are very good actors. You may not be *sure* that I am in pain: perhaps I feel nothing at all, but am just pretending. The outward signs of pain – screaming, avoiding the source of the pain, moaning, cradling the painful part of the body and so on – can be present when I am not feeling pain, and can be absent when I am. But in general, you can be confident that I feel pain in the same sorts of circumstances that you do.

Do non-human animals feel pain? To judge whether I felt pain, you used certain kinds of evidence. You looked at what might have caused me pain and at how I reacted. You can look out for these same signs of pain in an animal. Some things are obviously likely to cause an animal pain – getting an electric shock, getting scratched or bitten – and animals react to these in the same ways that humans react to painful stimuli: they avoid the source of the pain, they cry out, they nurse the damaged part of their body and so on.

Physiologically, some animals, especially higher mammals, have similar nervous systems to us, and they respond as we do when they are in the kind of circumstances in which we would feel pain: their blood pressure rises, their pulse rate increases, their pupils dilate, glands in their brains secrete chemicals that we know act as painkillers. Many animals react to pharmaceutical painkillers like opiates in the same way that we do; that is why it is often helpful to test them on animals.

The evidence that animals feel pain is similar to the evidence that other humans feel pain. Of course there is a difference between humans and animals: you can *ask* me whether I am in pain, and I can *tell* you; animals cannot. Is this difference important? It does not seem likely that having language is crucial, or very small babies who could not talk would never feel pain either. Of course, it is harder to tell what animals are feeling, since it is harder for them to communicate with us. But we should not *deny* that animals feel pain just because they cannot tell us that they do.

What about animals that are less similar to us than mammals? Can we tell if and when they are in pain? If their 'pain behaviour' is not the same as ours, that is, if there are no changes to their pulse rate or blood pressure, and they do not cry out, flinch or avoid sources of pain, it is harder to judge whether they feel any pain. Some creatures are biologically quite different from us and it is harder to say whether they have evolved so that they can experience pain. Reptiles and fish do not have nervous systems like ours, but they respond in ways that look like they are experiencing 'alarm', 'aggravation' and 'stress'. Crustaceans react as if they feel pain, though again, they have a very different nervous system from ours. Can these creatures feel anything? Or are they responding to stimuli without feeling anything at all?

Even advocates of animal liberation draw a line between animals they think feel pain and animals they think do not. Peter Singer is certain that mammals feel pain, is fairly confident that fish do, but strongly suspects that primitive organisms such as molluscs do not.

Natural Selection

Humans are biologically similar to other animals, and as Darwin's theory of evolution tells us, all the species that now exist, including humans, evolved from common ancestors. Consequently, it would be surprising if humans were unique in being the only species to be conscious and capable of feeling pain.

On the other hand, it is quite possible for one species to have characteristics that it does not share with any other. It is reasonable to think that humans are the only creatures currently capable of building rockets that can fly to the moon. No matter how biologically similar we are to other animals, they do not share all of our abilities. It may seem arbitrary to draw a line between humans and other animals, and claim that only we are conscious. But presumably there must be some line dividing conscious and non-conscious creatures, and wherever it is drawn will seem arbitrary.

Though Darwin's theory does not prove that animals other than humans are conscious, it gives us good reasons to think that they may be. According to the theory of evolution, each new generation of animals is 'copied' from their parents with a few small changes, or 'mutations'. The 'fittest' creatures, those best able to reproduce in their environment, are more likely to survive and have offspring. If an animal has some feature that makes it better able to survive and reproduce, after a long time, more of its descendants with copies of its genes will live than descendants of animals without it. It is useful for a gazelle to be able to run fast to escape from its predators. Gazelles that can run fast survive for longer and reproduce more often than slower gazelles; eventually there are more fast gazelles (descended from successful faster gazelles) than slow gazelles (descended from less successful slower gazelles). If a conscious animal were better able to survive and reproduce than a non-conscious animal, we would expect that after a time, the species would evolve so that all the members of that species were conscious. Presumably our ancestors who were conscious and could feel pain were more successful than their non-conscious brethren, and as a consequence our species evolved so that all humans are conscious.

Pain has the effect of making us avoid things that can injure us, which is surely likely to enhance our success at survival and reproduction. If an animal can feel pain, and so avoid dangers that might harm it, that animal's chances of survival are good. It is likely that animals that evolved to have a nervous system physiologically similar to ours did so for the same reason that we did. It would be very surprising if humans were the only kind of animal that evolved to feel pain: we should expect that non-human animals, especially those with a similar nervous system to ours, feel pain too.

This argument assumes that pain has a useful function, and that anything that has such a useful function is likely to have evolved in other animals as well as in humans. Both these assumptions have been questioned.

It is controversial whether pain, or more generally consciousness, has a useful function at all. Many philosophers think that only physical things, like states of the brain, can cause physical effects. If some state of your brain were to cause you to avoid dangerous things even when you did not feel pain, you would survive as well as a creature that avoids injury to avoid feeling pain.

Suppose that pain does have a useful function, encouraging one to avoid danger. Humans could still be the only species that has the capacity to feel it. It is possible that conscious creatures have evolved so recently that there is only one species that feels pain. It is possible that in non-human animals feeling pain was useful in some respects but so costly in other ways that creatures that could feel pain were less 'fit' than other animals, and did not survive. But it is nevertheless likely that those creatures with a similar physiology to ours that exhibit 'pain behaviour' like ours can feel pain.

Should We Treat Animals as if They Feel Pain?

Like all our best scientific theories, our explanations of animal behaviour should be as simple as possible. If we do not need to assume that animals can feel pain, we should not do so.

This is a good principle when we are studying animals scientifically, and trying to find out if they do have mental states, and if so, what kinds of minds they have.

But is it equally good when we think about ethics, about how we ought to treat animals? There might be some animals that can feel pain even though we have little evidence that they do, because their physiology is totally unlike our own and their behaviour in response to pain is quite different. If we used the principle *assume that nothing has a mind unless you have evidence that it does*, we might well conclude that these creatures could not feel pain and that we could treat them how we liked. But these creatures might suffer just as terribly as an animal that we knew could feel pain. No animal feels any less pain just because we do not know about it.

Perhaps this principle is fine for science, but won't do for ethics. We should be more cautious in ethics, and try to avoid causing pain to any animal that *might* be conscious. Perhaps in ethics we should accept the principle: *assume that everything has a mind unless you have evidence it doesn't*.

But if we accepted that principle, we would have to assume that trees, shrubs and computers might be conscious and would have to be very careful not to cause them to suffer, for what evidence do we have that they have no minds? This is plainly ridiculous: even in ethics, we need not assume that just anything might be conscious and capable of suffering. We should reject the second principle. So how should we treat animals?

We should distinguish between different kinds of animal. Where there is any evidence that animals can feel pain, we should be prepared to assume that they do. We should be confident that those animals that have a similar physiology to us and that act in ways that we recognise as expressing pain, can feel pain. It is very likely that mammals, having a similar physiology to us, feel pain like we do. It is quite likely that fish that respond to painful stimuli in ways we recognise as 'pain behaviour' also can feel pain. It is possible, though far less certain, that simple creatures like molluscs feel pain.

Though we should be wary of attributing consciousness too broadly, we can be confident that many animals can feel pain. But humans can suffer in other ways as well, that are not directly connected with feeling pain. We suffer from fear, anxiety and distress; do animals too?

Fear, Anxiety and Distress

Fear is an emotional response to danger; it is unpleasant but it enables us to prepare ourselves: to face up to the danger or to flee as fast as we can. Anxiety is also a response to a perceived threat, but whereas fear is focussed specifically on the danger, anxiety is a more general feeling of unease.

There is good behavioural evidence that some animals feel fear and anxiety. In situations that are likely to produce anxiety, for example when rats are randomly given electric shocks, the animals behave similarly to anxious humans: their pulse rate and respiration quicken, they sweat, their normal behaviour is inhibited, they tense up and are 'hyper-attentive' to their surroundings, constantly looking round for danger. If an anxious rat is given anti-anxiety drugs, its behaviour returns to normal.

We can use the same Darwinian arguments that we used for pain to explain why other animals might feel fear and anxiety. Fear and anxiety are useful to us because they prepare us to deal with a potential threat: we are alert and ready. It would be surprising if humans were the only species to have evolved with these useful emotions; it is far more likely that some other species – perhaps only mammals, perhaps fish too – have developed the same responses.

Distress or suffering is the experience of pain, fear, anxiety or other unpleasant feelings at a significant level. Animals can suffer distress just as we can, and in similar ways. But if we want to take account of animal suffering, we need to have some way of telling not just that animals *can* feel fear and pain, but *how unpleasant* their experiences really are. We know that it is difficult to tell even of other humans what they are feeling: how can we measure distress in animals?

The best guide to animal distress is how well the animal is coping with its environment. An animal fails to cope with its environment if it falls ill, is injured, exhibits behaviour associated with fear, anxiety or pain (raised heartbeat, sweating), and so on. This measure is obviously at best a crude rough guide, because it is difficult to compare these different 'symptoms', and it is hard to know how much an animal that fails to cope in these ways actually feels distress. But this is the most satisfactory current method of comparing, for example, the distress suffered by animals in

A caged primate in a laboratory © Brian Gunn / IAAPEA

different kinds of farming. Factory-farmed animals are frequently injured or ill and have difficulty breathing and moving around, free-range farmed animals are less often ill and injured and are able to express their natural behaviour. Free-range farmed animals cope much better with their environment than factory-farmed animals do, so we can say that factory-farmed animals tend to suffer much more than free-range farmed animals.

CHAPTER FOUR

CAN THEY REASON?

The Call of the Wild, by Jack London, reputedly the most-read American novel of all time, tells the story of Buck, a dog kidnapped from his comfortable family home and forced to pull a sled through the frozen Klondike during the gold-rush. Buck, bred from a huge St Bernard, survives and even thrives in his new life, in part through his immense size and strength, but also through a mixture of instinct and intelligence. Buck is a fighter and a killer. He enjoys the taste of blood. But when it comes to a battle to the death with his great rival, Spitz, he does not rely solely on his instincts: feinting as if to shoulder-charge, instead he bites the other dog's front legs, breaking them and leaving him helpless. Buck wins because he is thoughtful and cunning, as well as vicious and powerful.

Jack London's portrayal of the mind of a dog is certainly gripping, but is it at all realistic? We often interpret animals as having thoughts: the cat that stands by the door wants to go out; the excited dog thinks he is about to be taken for a walk. We can tell that the dog is expecting to see his owner at the door, and is disappointed to find a stranger instead. We interpret a dog as burying the bone so that he can dig it up and enjoy it later. But we also know that, like Buck, many animals act on instinct, without thinking about what they are doing and why. For example, many animals salivate when they get food, without believing that salivating helps them to get food or to digest it.

If you have a belief, you represent the world to yourself in a particular way: if you believe that it is sunny, you represent that the sun is shining; if you think it is raining, you represent the world differently. You choose what to do on the basis of your beliefs: if you want to sunbathe, you go outside when you think that it is sunny, and stay indoors when you think that it is not.

In the last chapter we saw that behaviourists thought that it was a mistake to attribute any mental states to animals; they would describe an animal's outward behaviour – the cat has moved closer to the door and is vocalising – but they would not explain this in terms of mental states. They thought that saying *the cat wants to go outside* was hopelessly anthropomorphic.

Behaviourists tried to explain animal behaviour in purely non-mental terms. But it proved difficult if not impossible to understand animals without describing them as having desires and beliefs. As soon as we accept that the cat *wants* to go out, we know why she is standing by the door; for a behaviourist, it is a mystery. It is not anthropomorphic to think that animals have minds: it is simple common sense.

Of course, it is *possible* that only humans have a mental life whereas all other animals act only on instinct. But just as it would be surprising if humans but no other animals, no matter how biologically similar, were conscious and could feel pain, it would be surprising if humans had thoughts and desires but no other animals did. Having beliefs and desires rather than mere instincts is useful to us, enabling us to represent the world in ways that it could be but is not, in ways that we would like it to be; we can begin to think not just about how the world is but about how we might change it. Having beliefs as well as instincts is likely to give any animal an evolutionary advantage, helping it live for longer and reproduce more successfully, so we should expect that at least some other animals have thoughts as well as instincts.

But we still need to make sure that we are not being anthropomorphic, ascribing beliefs and desires inappropriately all over the place. It seems natural for us to describe some animals at least as having beliefs and desires. But it also seems to be natural for us to talk about the beliefs and desires of many things, not all of which have minds. We say that plants like to be watered and to grow towards the light. We say that a thermostat wants the room to be at 22 degrees, so it turns on the heating until it thinks that the room is at that temperature, and then turns it off.

The philosopher Dan Dennett calls this taking the 'intentional stance' towards thermostats and plants. When we take the intentional stance towards an object we explain its behaviour and predict what it will do in the future in terms of its goals and how it thinks it can achieve them: the thermostat's goal is to keep the room at a particular temperature, and it thinks it can achieve this by altering the heating.

It can be useful to take the intentional stance towards animals, describing their behaviour in terms of beliefs and desires, but it can be useful to take the intentional stance towards plants and thermostats, too, and we are pretty sure that plants and thermostats do not really have beliefs and desires: in fact, they have no minds at all. So we should be wary of assuming that animals have beliefs and desires, just because it is useful for us to talk about them as if they do.

Beliefs vs. Instinctive Responses to Stimuli

We know that sometimes animals react instinctively to stimuli, and that we can affect responses to stimuli by conditioning, that is, by repeatedly reinforcing with rewards a new response. But if we find out that an animal has reacted instinctively, we no longer think that it has acted on beliefs and desires. How is action based on beliefs and desires different from instinctive behaviour?

Action based on beliefs and desires is 'intelligently' flexible in a way that instinctive reactions to stimuli are not. Your actions are intelligently flexible in this sense: if you find that one way of pursuing your goal is no good, you will try to find another way of achieving it; you respond appropriately to relevant changes in your information. For example, if you want to get some bread, and you think that you can get some from the local bakery, you go there first of all. But if you find that it has sold out, you visit the out-of-town supermarket instead. If the first way you try to get your loaf fails, you adapt by finding a new means to your goal.

Also, you can use the same means to achieve a different goal: while you are at the supermarket, you may buy some vegetables too.

After repeated 'reinforcements', rats can be taught to press a bar in order to get food. It may seem that they are acting on beliefs and desires: the desire to get food and a belief that pressing the bar will get them it. But the rats' response is not flexible. If the experimenter changes the trial so that the rats do *not* get fed when they press the bar, the rats carry on pressing. They do not respond appropriately to changes in their situation.

The sphex wasp is another creature whose instincts are not intelligently flexible. The wasp lays eggs in a burrow, and leaves a stunned locust there for her offspring to eat when they hatch. She drags the locust to her burrow, goes in alone to check that it is free of intruders, and then drags the locust inside. The wasp seems to be acting on the desire to protect her offspring from predators and the belief that she can help protect them by carefully checking her burrow.

But if, while the wasp is inside checking her burrow, someone moves the locust away from its edge, when she goes back outside, she moves the locust back to the edge and checks inside again. And if it is moved again while she is inside, she does exactly the same again. And again. She does not ever recognise that she has already checked the burrow and has no need to do so once more. She acts on instinct, not on beliefs and desires.

A thermostat set to 22 degrees turns on the central heating when it registers the room temperature as less than

22 degrees, and turns it off when it registers that the temperature has reached that figure. It is not flexible; it cannot aim at different goals, and it can only regulate the temperature in one way. If the link between the thermostat and the heating breaks, the thermostat cannot respond; it cannot cool the room by opening a window instead, for example.

Agents who act on their beliefs and desires are able to choose the same means to achieve different goals, and different means for the same aim, depending on their circumstances; whereas thermostats are designed to pursue one goal, and always to pursue it in the same way. Many animals make conditioned responses to stimuli, some of which, like a dog salivating before it is fed, are extremely simple. But it is not just because they are simple that these behaviours do not count as action based on beliefs and desires. The instincts of the sphex wasp are quite complex and sophisticated. Instinctive and conditioned responses to stimuli are different from action based on beliefs and desires because they are inflexible, not because they are less complicated. But are any animals capable of intelligent action based on beliefs and desires rather than mere responses to stimuli?

The Link between Language and Belief

We know that humans are intelligent agents because we talk to each other: using a complex language is a clear sign of intelligent thought. Many people who insist that animals have no beliefs do so on the basis that animals do not use language. On the other hand, if we found that some animals were language-users, we could be fairly certain that they were capable of thought too. So it is crucial whether animals do in fact use language. One might have thought that this was a pretty straightforward issue to settle, but in fact it turns out to be extremely controversial.

Animals certainly communicate with one another. Many animals mark off territory using smells (for example urine) sometimes described as a 'signature'. Other animals tend to keep out of the territory once they have noticed the scent.

When bees find a large supply of nectar, they fly back to the nest and perform a 'dance' which encodes information about the direction and distance of the food. Other bees that see the dance use this information to find the nectar.

What is notable about these signs is that each time, similar information is encoded in a similar sign. Bees communicate the whereabouts of a source of nectar by dancing in a particular way. They do not have different ways of encoding information about nectar sources in different styles of dancing, and they do not express different information in their dance, for example, about how they are feeling that day. The same is true of urine 'signatures'; they can only be used to say that this is some creature's territory.

Our use of language is much more flexible: we express all sorts of information in all sorts of different ways, we have many different ways of saying the same thing and we can put into words lots of different ideas. And the way we use language to communicate is very complicated.

Suppose I say to you: 'This is my land.' There is a convention among speakers of English that the words I have used mean that this piece of land belongs to me. We both know this, and we both know that the other knows it. When I say, 'This is my land', I intend that you form the belief that the land is mine, because you recognise that I said what I did *so that* you would form that very belief. Any communication of this kind requires the speaker to have quite complex intentions and beliefs. And similarly the interpreter needs to know not just what the words mean, but also that the speaker has those beliefs and intentions.

When animals leave behind 'urine signatures', are they communicating in this complex way? They might be, but they are probably doing something much more simple. Animals may simply produce urine signatures and other animals avoid them without thinking at all: such instincts would keep potentially dangerous rival animals away from one another, and so are likely to be selected by evolution. The animals themselves may have absolutely no idea what they are doing. They certainly need not attribute beliefs or intentions to other creatures; the system of 'signatures' may be totally different from human communication.

No other animal naturally uses a language anywhere near as complex as human languages; it used to be thought that animals were incapable of doing so. But there have been more or less successful attempts to encourage chimps, gorillas and other higher apes to learn sign language. Washoe and Nim Chimpski were among the first chimps to be taught sign language intensively.

It is controversial how far these chimps mastered sign language; sceptics think that the claims made by their trainers are much too generous. Chimps can clearly understand words for material objects (head, nut, cat), and simple commands (fetch, put), but in other respects their language use falls a long way short of normal human use, even that of young children. They rarely start conversations or produce novel sentences, as human infants do. Though chimps can produce simple sentences, they do not appear to be able to talk about the future and have trouble mastering complex concepts, such as conditionals (sentences like: if X, then Y) and causation (sentences like: X causes Y).

The difference between human and ape language use is well illustrated by an unlikely encounter that took place between William Shatner, the actor well known for playing Captain James T. Kirk of *Star Trek*, and Koko, a signing gorilla. Shatner muses on the significance of the meeting:

> Koko and I talked. We touched hands and we touched minds. Feeling her powerful hand on the back of my neck was unlike any experience I've known. ... The hand across the border that Koko extended to me taught me in that one moment that we are linked inexorably with everything else in nature and that for us to be destroying species after species is criminal.

Koko's concerns, as expressed in a conversation with her trainer, Dr Francine 'Penny' Patterson, are more straightforward:

Candy give-me
Drink apple
Sleep lie-down. This red red hurry.

Whereas Shatner expresses abstract ideas like the problematic relationship between man and nature in quite complex sentences, Koko talks about her immediate environment, what she sees and what she wants, in the simplest of terms.

It is clearly wrong to say that no animals are capable of language use. Many animals encode information in signs, and other animals respond to that information, as when creatures make urine 'signatures'. But it is certainly true that few animals, perhaps only chimps, perhaps higher apes, are capable of anything like human language use; most animals, including common domestic and farm animals such as cats, cows and chickens, are not capable of this at all. Even chimps do not seem to be able to use human language in ways as complex as human infants.

Much animal communication may be instinctive, rather than intelligently flexible action. But we should not conclude that animals cannot think just because they do not use language as we do. Perhaps their beliefs and ability to reason are shown in other contexts.

Surprise!

When you go to the local bakery and find that it has sold out, you are surprised. Your reaction is a sign that you have noticed that the world is different from the way you had represented it: you had represented the bakery as having bread you could buy; but in the real world, it has none.

If an animal were surprised when faced with an unexpected situation, we would have evidence that it had beliefs representing the world and was puzzled that the world differed from its representation. We might be able to tell that an animal was surprised or had changed its plans, even though, unlike another human, it could not tell us about it. One reason why we are confident that the sphex wasp acts on instinct rather than on beliefs is that she does *not* show any surprise when the locust is constantly moved away from her burrow.

We do have some evidence, if anecdotal, that animals do show surprise and do change their plans. A cat goes to the place it is normally fed, and finding no food there, goes to find her owner to complain about it. She planned to eat food from her dish, but when she realised that the dish was empty, she changed her mind. Unfortunately, it is always going to be hard to tell whether a cat was genuinely surprised at the lack of food or has merely learnt a complex response: when hungry, go to dish; if no food in dish, go to owner. But by careful observation of their behaviour, we have some evidence that animals do have beliefs.

The Content of Animal Beliefs

It is no good saying: animals must have beliefs, but of course I have absolutely no idea what they are. Suppose that Rover's owner is Mr Peter Jones. Does Rover believe he will be taken for a walk by his owner? Or by Mr Peter Jones? Or by a tall thing with a particular smell? Each of these is a different thought. If Rover can think, he must have beliefs that are about his master, or Peter Jones, or some completely different things. But how can we tell whether Rover thinks of Peter Jones as *my owner*, or as *someone called Peter Jones*? Unless we know this, we cannot have any precise idea of the content of his beliefs, and unless we have a good idea of their contents, we cannot really ascribe any beliefs to him at all.

We have a similar problem in knowing exactly what beliefs other humans have. For example, we may not be sure whether Peter Jones thinks *I will take Rover for a walk*, or *I will take my smelly dog for a walk*. He may think both at once. But it is easy to find out about Peter Jones's beliefs: we can ask him and he can tell us. Obviously we cannot ask the dog what he was thinking, so it is very much harder for us to work out what beliefs Rover has.

On the other hand, if we watch Rover carefully, we should be able to get a rough idea of what he believes. For example, Rover chews bones and buries them in the garden; he does not chew or bury anything else there. It is reasonable to think that Rover has beliefs about bones, like *there are some bones buried in the garden*. Of course, he may have a very different idea of bones than we do, his 'concept' of a bone may be quite unlike ours; he probably does not know that both he and his owner have bones inside them as part of their skeleton, for example. But it is reasonable to use our own words to describe Rover's beliefs, provided we keep in mind that his concepts are likely to differ from our own.

Conclusion

All of us describe animal behaviour in terms of beliefs and desires. Are we just hopelessly anthropomorphic? Some animals seem to act flexibly in response to changes in the world around them. It is always difficult to tell whether these animals have merely learnt complex responses to stimuli, but we have evidence that these behaviours are not mere instincts or conditioned responses if the animals show surprise that the world is not as they thought it was and seem to change their mind about what to do next.

Even if we are confident that these animals do have beliefs, it is very difficult for us to discover what they are thinking about. We can get a reasonable idea of exactly what beliefs dogs have by closely observing their behaviour, seeing whether they distinguish between cats and other kinds of animals they can chase, bones and other kinds of things they can eat. We can use our own concepts to describe doggie thoughts, but we must use caution, as dogs are likely to employ much less sophisticated concepts than we do, and may use different ones entirely; we must be aware that what we can say about the content of their beliefs is certainly limited and may be completely wrong. Nevertheless, careful observation of non-human animals can tell us that some of these creatures have beliefs and can give us an idea of what beliefs they have.

CHAPTER FIVE

ANIMAL INTELLIGENCE AND HUMAN MINDS

Clever Hans was a horse who lived in the 19th century. If you put a number of objects in front of him and asked him how many there were, he would tap out the answer with his hoof. Many people believed that Hans the horse could count, especially when they saw that he did not rely on clues about the right answer from his trainer; he could get the answer right even when his trainer was not around.

Hans the horse could not count. When he tapped his hoof, he was not counting out the number of objects in front of him, instead, he was responding to the excitement from people watching when he had tapped out the right number. If no one who could count was present, there was no excitement, and Hans kept on tapping his hoof: he did not know when to stop. At first, it looked as if Hans was an extraordinary horse who genuinely could understand numbers. In fact, he was indeed exceptional, but in his sensitivity to people's reactions to him, not because he had outstanding abilities at maths. Hans was clever, but not in the way that his 19th-century fans thought he was.

Sometimes animals fool us into thinking that they are intelligent when they are not. At first glance, we are impressed with the foresight and care of the sphex wasp, checking her burrow for predators before bringing in food for her offspring. But we soon find out that she is not as clever as she seems: she always does the same thing, whether or not she has good reason. The sphex wasp and Clever Hans show us that we need to be very careful of jumping to conclusions about animal intelligence: we must be wary of anthropomorphism, of assuming that animal minds are exactly like ours.

In the past there have been many attempts to draw a clear line between human and animal minds, to discover which of our abilities are distinctively human. Perhaps only humans can use language? But as we saw in the last chapter, many animals communicate with one another and some higher apes are able to learn simple human languages. Perhaps only humans are self-aware, or have culture, or can use tools: is there anything we can do that animals can't?

Use of Tools and Tool-making

In the past, many people thought that using tools was a distinctively human activity. Of course, many of the animals with which we are most familiar – dogs, cats, pigs, cows and sheep – do not use tools at all. But eventually we discovered that several other species of animal do: some chimps use stones to break up nuts, some use sticks to poke into ants' nests to help them eat the ants. Egyptian vultures use stones to break open eggshells; song thrushes carry snails high into the air and drop them to smash on the rocks below.

The ability to use tools is obviously not unique to humans, for many animals use tools too, but perhaps they cannot *make* tools. After all, using tools may not be a sign of great intelligence, for one might stumble over an appropriate stone or twig and accidentally use it in the right way. Making a tool, by contrast, seems to involve considerably more thought. Suppose that you are a chimp and you would like to eat some ants that are hiding in their nest. You can pick up ants individually by hand, but that's a very slow process. You realise that if you poke a stick into the nest, the ants cling on to it, so that when you pull it out of the nest, you can feast on the ants. But you need the right kind of stick, one that you can easily poke into the nest and get out again: you need a long stick without any side-branches. You find a stick of a suitable length and pull away the side-branches and leaves. Now it's a perfect tool to pick up ants; all you need now is to find a nest and you can eat as much as you want. And in fact, this is exactly what ant-eating chimps do.

If the chimps were really clever, they might be able to design tools in the abstract: they might be able to think up the ideal ant-eating stick by thinking about what they want the tool for, without trying out different sizes and shapes of twig. If not, they could find the ideal tool by testing lots of different types of stick, seeing which worked best, then modifying other twigs to look like their best effort.

It is not clear whether chimps can design tools in the abstract or whether they merely find the best tools by trial and error. But in either case, tool-making is not a distinctively human ability, for chimps at least can do so as well.

Cultured Creatures

Animals both use and make tools: these abilities do not distinguish humans from other animals. But there may be other distinctively human capacities; perhaps humans are unlike other animals because only humans have culture.

We have many practices that we could have carried out differently: everyone in our society talks in the same language, but we all could have preferred a different one; everyone drives on one side of the road, but we could have chosen the other side. We learn our language and driving skills from other humans in our society: no one is born knowing English or which way to point their car. Culture, understood in this broad sense, is a huge influence on us; what we learn in our society affects enormously how we live our lives.

Do animals have culture? There is evidence that at least some animals do have practices that are not biologically determined but that are spread through social learning. There is a troop of macaques (a kind of monkey) living on the Pacific island of Koshima that wash sweet potatoes in the sea before they eat them. Researchers who studied the monkeys left the potatoes on the beach for them, and initially, the macaques would eat them without washing them. One day one of the macaques washed her potato in the sea, and soon all the other animals in the troop copied

Animal culture: a macaque washing a potato
© Heather Angel/Natural Visions

her and washed their potatoes too. Young macaques were taught the practice and it was passed on to the next generation. Similarly, chimps that use stones to break the shells off nuts do not need to work out what is the best shape of stone by trial and error; they copy chimps that already know what to do. Like humans, many apes are very good at imitating what another is doing; this enables them to learn from one another, so it is not surprising that apes as well as humans have culture, at least of a simple kind.

Some animals have shown a surprising sensitivity to the higher forms of human culture too. There are many anecdotes of animals enjoying Mozart's music, and scientists have discovered that sparrows tend to prefer listening to Bach than to Schönberg. Pigeons were even proved by Tokyo scientist Shigeru Watanabe to be extremely discerning art critics. Birds were trained with rewards to peck at copies of either Picasso's or Monet's paintings. They were then presented with another set of pictures, which they had never seen before. The pigeons were able to pick out works by the artists they had been trained to recognise, even when the pictures were entirely new to them. And when presented with paintings by artists of a similar period, the Picasso-trained birds preferred other cubists, whereas birds trained on Monet preferred other impressionists like Renoir. Amazingly, pigeons can apparently distinguish different schools of art as well as work by different painters. It seems that even appreciation of art and music is not distinctive of our species.

Can Animals Think About Themselves?

Do animals have a sense of self? If we held up a mirror to a cat or a dog, would it recognise itself?

Gordon Gallup, an animal researcher, decided to take this question literally, and test whether chimpanzees could recognise themselves reflected in a mirror. To start with, the chimps treated their reflection in the same way as they would another chimp: they stared at it, cautiously approached it and looked behind the mirror. Afterwards, they used the mirror to look at the inside of their mouths and parts of their body they had not seen before. To test whether the chimps really did realise that they were looking at themselves, Gallup put them under anaesthetic and painted a red mark on their faces. When the chimps woke up and each saw himself in the mirror, he touched the red mark on his face much more than he normally would; some chimps touched the mark and then looked at their fingers. Gallup's experiment suggests that chimps do recognise themselves in the mirror, and further experiments show that orang-utans, bonobos and human children who are over the age of two do too. Monkeys, by contrast, do not seem to pass the test, for they do not touch the red mark on their face when they see themselves in the mirror.

The significance of Gallup's experiments is hotly debated. Gallup thought he had shown that chimps were self-aware because they could recognise themselves in the mirror. Is the test definitive of self-awareness: if monkeys fail the test, must we conclude that they are not self-aware? No. Monkeys and other animals might fail the test even if they are aware of themselves because the test is not well designed for them. For some species of monkey, staring at another monkey is a sign of aggression, so many monkeys do not look closely at their mirror image for fear of starting a fight with a potential rival. They may not recognise themselves because they are not willing to stare into the mirror, rather than because they are not self-aware.

Of course, if chimps do recognise themselves in the mirror, they must be able to think: *That's me!* And Gallup's experiment suggests they are also thinking: *What's that strange mark on my head?* But it does not show that they have any more awareness of themselves than that: chimps may not be aware of their own thoughts or feelings.

Humans are self-aware in the further sense that we can reflect on what we are thinking. *That was a clever idea of mine*, I think smugly to myself, as I turn down a side-street to make a short-cut to the shops. *No, it was really stupid*, I ruefully reflect, as I realise that I'm going to get stuck in the one-way system after all. I can think about my own beliefs, and assess them for being clever or stupid, reasonable or unreasonable, true or false.

I am also aware that I am a creature that exists through time: I vow that tomorrow, I won't take the wrong 'short-cut' and make the same mistake as I made yesterday. Self-awareness in humans involves more than just the ability to recognise oneself in the mirror. It includes *the ability to reflect on and assess your own thoughts*, and *the recognition that you existed in the past and will exist in the future*. Even if chimps are self-aware in the sense that they pass the mirror-recognition test, we cannot tell from that test whether they have these extra abilities that humans have. And at the moment, we have no other evidence that they do.

The philosopher Donald Davidson, having assumed that animals cannot reflect on their own thoughts, has argued that they have no beliefs at all. He claims that to have beliefs at all, a creature has to be able to reflect on its beliefs and recognise that they are representations of the world that sometimes are accurate and sometimes are not. We are capable of this kind of reflection, but we have no evidence that animals are; Davidson concludes that animals probably have no beliefs. But it is obviously one thing to represent the world in a certain way and to act on that basis, for example, to represent a tree as having bananas in it, to climb the tree and eat the bananas; it is quite another to recognise that you have represented the world in a certain way, and that your representation might be inaccurate, to recognise that though you *think* there are bananas in the tree, there might *not* be. Davidson is wrong: if you represent the world and act on that basis, you have beliefs, whether or not you realise that you might have got the world completely wrong. Even if animals cannot think about themselves as we humans do, they may still have beliefs.

Can Animals Understand Other Minds?

Do any other animals have beliefs about the minds of other animals? Can they tell what other animals are thinking? There is evidence that they may do: animals have been observed apparently trying to deceive one another. An ape that is not badly hurt may go about limping so that the others share food with him and generally treat him better: he seems to be deceiving other apes for his own benefit. But does the ape pretend to limp because he believes that other apes will *think* that he is injured and feel sorry for him? Or does he merely discover by trial and error that he gets more food when he limps? He might limp because he gets more food that way, without making any assumptions about what the other apes think about him.

How can we tell whether animals think about what other animals are thinking? The 'false belief test' has been devised to find out whether human children can 'mind-read', that is, to find out whether they can work out what other humans are thinking. Normal children can 'mind-read' from the age of four or five.

A modified version of the false belief test has been devised to test whether animals (often chimps) can ascribe beliefs to others. In the first test, a chimp is shown two opaque boxes, which are then hidden from her view. One researcher (the hider) hides a reward in one box, while another (the communicator) watches. The chimp can see that the communicator knows in which box the reward is hidden, but she does not know the right box herself. The chimp can then choose between the two boxes; the communicator points to the right box; when the chimp chooses it, she gets the reward.

Once the chimp has learnt to choose the box indicated by the communicator, the set-up is changed. In the next trial, the hider hides the reward while the communicator watches. The chimp still cannot see the chosen box and can still observe that the communicator knows which it is. Next, the communicator leaves the room, while the hider switches round the boxes. The communicator returns and indicates the box that he *thinks* contains the reward (which of course is empty). If the chimp realises that the communicator is indicating the wrong box (because he does not know that the boxes have been switched), the chimp should choose the *other* box. Children over five realise that the communicator has a *false belief* about the whereabouts of the reward, and pass the test. No chimp has yet passed the test.

A second version of the false belief test has been designed to see whether chimps can ascribe beliefs to other chimps, rather than to humans. First of all, food is hidden in front of both subordinate and dominant chimps. The dominant chimp gets most of this food. Next, food is hidden in front of subordinate chimps when the dominant chimp cannot see what is going on. The subordinate chimp can see where the food is hidden and that the dominant chimp does not know where the food is. The subordinate chimp waits until the dominant chimp is out of the way, then gets the food and eats it herself. In this test, subordinate chimps act differently depending on whether they think that a dominant chimp knows about the hidden food; they must be mind-reading.

Chimps that failed the first version of the false belief test can pass the second test; they seem to be able to 'mind-read' in some circumstances but not others. Perhaps they find it easier to think about what other chimps believe, rather than creatures of another species. Perhaps they are more used to competition than co-operation, and so are better at thinking, as in the second test, about the beliefs of animals that are competing with them for food, rather than, as in the first test, about the beliefs of creatures that are co-operating with them.

Very few animals other than higher apes and dolphins have passed any false belief test, but this does not prove that none of them can 'mind-read': we may simply have failed to design a test that proves that they can. Alternatively, an animal could be aware of its own beliefs as mental representations of the world, while assuming that no other creature had a mind at all: it might be able to reflect on its own beliefs, though it always failed a false belief test. The experiments show that at least chimps, dolphins and some other animals do have a partial grasp of what a belief is, for they attribute beliefs to other creatures in some circumstances.

Autonomous Action and Morality

Many people have tried to draw a line between humans and animals, claiming that only humans use tools, or make tools, or have culture, or use language, or have beliefs about other minds. But at least chimps and other higher apes are to some degree like humans in these respects; they use language and tools and pass some versions of the false belief test. Human and animal minds are different only in degree, not in kind. But though human and animal intelligence are on a continuum, the differences between them can still be important.

A cat sees a mouse running across a field. She crouches near to the ground ready to spring. When the mouse trots nearby, she pounces on him, kills him and eats him.

This cat, like many animals, decides what to do on the basis of its beliefs and desires. How is this different from the way that humans act? Often, we just act on our beliefs and desires too. But we can also reflect on whether acting on our beliefs and desires is really a good idea.

Suppose that I want to buy some new clothes to follow the latest fashions, and also to give some money to charity to help people in need. I could just act on these desires: go to the shops and choose some new clothes; send off a cheque to the charity. I am free to do what I want: there is nothing to stop me doing either. If I simply did what I wanted, I would be a free agent, just as animals are free agents when they act on their beliefs and desires. But sometimes I *reflect* on my desires and see whether I *really* want to have those desires, whether I think that acting on them is really *worthwhile*. When I reflect on my desire to give to charity, I think that it's good to have such desires and act on them, so I go and give money to the charity. When I think about my desire to have fashionable clothes, I am not sure that it's good that I have such desires. I have perfectly good clothes already; why should I care about whether what I'm wearing is fashionable? Isn't it rather shallow – and expensive – to follow such trends?

We are capable of reflecting on our beliefs and desires, and on why we have them. We can assess whether we have good reasons for them: is a desire to be fashionable harmless or shallow? And sometimes we alter our beliefs, desires and behaviour in line with what we think are good reasons: I change my mind about going shopping because I decide that it's silly to want new clothes all the time; instead I stay at home and write out a cheque to Oxfam. This capacity to reflect on our desires, to assess whether we have genuine reasons for them, and to choose whether or not actually to act on them is our capacity to be *autonomous*. 'Autonomous' means 'self-governing': we are self-governing because we are not slaves to our own desires. We can reflect on whether our desires are worthwhile; we can choose to act on desires that seem to us to be good and choose not to act on desires that seem worthless or bad.

The cat catches the mouse because she wants to eat it. Animals act on their beliefs and desires, but as far as we know, they do not think about their beliefs, desires and actions and assess them as we do. The cat may think about how she can best stalk the mouse, but she does not wonder whether she ought not to eat it in the first place. Though we know that some animals, like the higher apes, have a partial concept of belief and can think about the minds of some other animals, we have no evidence that any animals reflect on whether they have good reasons to do what they want, whether it would be better if they had different desires or did something else. We have no evidence that animals are autonomous.

Moral Responsibility

When we catch Bob the burglar red-handed inside someone else's house with a bag of swag, we hold him responsible for breaking the law and acting wrongly. He is dishonest: he deserves criticism, blame and punishment for what he has done. Even if he had never thought about whether a life of crime was wrong, he could have done, he could have chosen not to become a burglar. Even if in fact no career path except burglary ever occurred to him, he should have known better.

When a human does something wrong, we hold them responsible for what they have done, except in special circumstances. If Bob were a kleptomaniac, or under hypnosis, or if he had taken mind-altering drugs, we would treat him quite differently: he would need treatment for his problems rather than blame and punishment. If Bob were a child, we would try to teach him not to break the law and act dishonestly, but we do not hold children responsible for wrong-doing in the same way as adults: children need to learn what is right and wrong, adults should know.

When we hold Bob responsible for his crime, we treat him as a *moral agent*: someone who acts well or badly, who deserves praise or blame and punishment. We do not treat drug addicts or kleptomaniacs as moral agents because they cannot properly reflect on whether they are acting for good or bad reasons, and even if they do recognise that they are acting for bad reasons, there is typically nothing they can do about it: if a drug-addict realises he would be better off not addicted to the drug, it is very difficult for him just to stop taking it. Drug addicts and kleptomaniacs are not fully in control of their thoughts and actions: they are not autonomous. That is why it is not appropriate to hold them morally responsible for what they do. We treat children as moral agents in the making: we try to teach them the difference between good and bad reasons for action, we correct them when they act wrongly so that they can learn to take responsibility for their actions.

We are autonomous; we can reflect on our reasons for action, decide whether they are good, and change our behaviour so that we act for good reasons. Animals are not autonomous; they are not able to reflect on why they do what they do. To be morally responsible you need to be able to assess your reasons for action: for example, you must be able to take into account the probable effects of your actions on others' feelings and on what they want. But very few animals have any idea what other animals think or feel. It is no surprise, therefore, that we do not treat animals as morally responsible for what they do. Though we may try to train them, altering their behaviour with rewards and punishments, we do not usually think that animals can be guilty of crimes or that they deserve blame or punishment. For example, though chimps and bonobos are biologically very closely related, their social groups are very different; chimps are much more aggressive and violent than bonobos, who usually resolve conflicts by having sex. But we would not conclude that chimps were morally worse as a species than bonobos: each acts in ways natural to them. Similarly, we would not judge the cat that catches and eats a mouse as guilty of murder; the cat is doing what is natural for her, and is not capable of wondering whether it is right or wrong.

Some animals, especially those like chimps who live in complex social groups, act in ways that we would call virtuous if we saw them in humans. Many of these animals look after their own young, sometimes they even care for the young of other animals and the old and frail members of their group; they seem to show sympathy and concern for others. Some animals have social networks where they reciprocally help one another. Vampire bats go out each night to find a meal of blood. When they return to their cave, the successful bats regurgitate some of the blood they have eaten to a bat that was not so lucky.

We may be tempted to call these bats altruistic, but we have no evidence that they think of what they are doing in moral terms. They may even be acting on instinct. Many animals may be capable of suffering from fear and anxiety, as we saw in Chapter 3, but there is little evidence that they can feel moral emotions like guilt and shame that are experienced only by those who have an understanding of moral right and wrong. As Mark Twain said, 'Man is the only animal that blushes. Or that needs to.'

Of course, we can say that certain animals are acting *like* someone who is generous or benevolent, but we should not praise them for acting well unless we are also prepared to hold responsible animals that seem selfish or violent. We cannot consistently praise bonobos for their peacefulness, unless we are prepared to blame chimps for their aggression, but it is surely grossly inappropriate to blame animals that are not capable of thinking about the right and wrong way to behave. Since animals are not autonomous, we ought not to treat them as morally responsible for their actions.

Conclusion

In Chapters 3 and 4 of his book *The Descent of Man*, Darwin wrote:

> There is no fundamental difference between man and the higher mammals in their mental faculties ... The lower animals, like man, manifestly feel pleasure and pain, happiness and misery ... There can be no doubt that the difference between the mind of the lowest man and that of the highest animal is immense ... Nevertheless, the difference in mind between man and the higher animals, great as it is, certainly is one of degree and not of kind.

As in many things, he was completely correct. Like us, many animals can feel pain; some also suffer from fear and anxiety. Some animals can form beliefs, and act on their beliefs and desires, rather than merely on instinct. The traditional ways of distinguishing man from the other animals – as a user of tools, or maker of tools, or user of language – all fail, because other animals are capable of these too.

Nevertheless, there are some important differences between human and animal minds. As far as we know, no animals are autonomous: they are not capable of reflecting on their beliefs and desires, of assessing whether they have good reasons to act, or of changing their behaviour in line with what they think they have most reason to do. As a consequence, no animals other than humans are morally responsible for what they do. This fact is obviously morally significant: it follows that man is the only animal that can be innocent or guilty and deserve punishment. But does it make a difference in other ways to the moral status of animals? This is a question for the next part of this book, where we consider whether animals have moral status, and whether they have rights.

PART TWO
ALL ANIMALS ARE
EQUAL …?

CHAPTER SIX

RIGHTS AND MORAL STATUS

'If you prick us, do we not bleed? If you tickle us, do we not laugh? If you poison us, do we not die? And if you wrong us, shall we not revenge?'

In *The Merchant of Venice*, Antonio borrows some money from Shylock, a Jew, agreeing to repay it by a certain date. But when the payment is due, he has lost his money and cannot keep his word. In these lines, Shylock argues that the harm Antonio has done to him matters morally, insisting that he must be allowed to extract compensation for the wrong he has suffered, just as a Christian would. In Shakespeare's play, his eloquent plea is accepted, though ultimately his legal case does not go as he had planned.

In arguing that the harm inflicted on him matters morally, Shylock is claiming that he has *moral status*. Our ordinary moral thought distinguishes humans, who have moral status, from things like stones and pieces of wood that do not. There is nothing morally wrong with treating an ordinary stone or a piece of wood – mere objects – in any way that you want. It does not matter morally if you smash them up or stamp on them just because you feel like it, and you have no reason to feel guilty for doing so. The value of an object depends on how useful it is to you: if you need a stone, that stone is valuable to you; when you no longer need it, it is worthless.

Unlike stones and pieces of wood, humans are capable of feeling pain and pleasure, and thinking about their own lives. It matters morally how you treat other humans: you ought not to harm them unnecessarily: you should not lie to them, steal from them, cheat them or kill them. When you think of doing something that might harm them, you ought to take into consideration the pain you might cause them and what *they* want to do with their life, as well as what you want for yourself. The value of humans does not depend on how useful they are.

Do animals have moral status like humans, or do they lack moral status like sticks and stones? Does it matter morally if you hurt a dog or a cat? What about slugs or toads, or bacteria?

Of course, what you do to animals or plants might matter morally because of the effects on those who own the animals or plants. I ought not to cut down your tree or kick your dog without your permission, because they are your property. But if a dog did not belong to anyone, or if it belonged to me, would it matter what I did to it?

In this and the following four chapters, I will try to decide whether animals, like people, have moral status. But first I want to distinguish the question of moral status from the question of whether animals have rights. There is enormous disagreement about what it means to have a right, whether humans have rights and what rights they have. But we cannot even begin to consider whether animals have rights before getting clear about what rights really are.

Legal Rights

You can have two different kinds of rights, legal rights and moral rights. You have a legal right if it follows from the law of your country that you are entitled to perform some action or to be treated by others in a particular way.

For example, you and I and the citizens of many countries have a legal right to freedom of speech, because we are entitled to express our opinions in any way we choose. You and I have a right to life, because no one may permissibly kill us. If some people try to prevent us from expressing our opinion, or if they try to kill us, they are breaking the law. We may bring them to trial and, if they are found guilty, they will be punished.

In the UK before 1822, animals had no legal rights. There were laws concerning animals, and some of those laws prohibited harming animals. But these laws treated animals as the property of people. Killing a farm animal was wrong in the same way that burning down a farmer's barn was wrong: it damaged his property. Because it was the farmer, the owner of the animal, who was protected by the law, he had rights concerning the animal, but the animal had no rights at all: someone who killed a chicken violated the rights of the owner of the chicken, but not the legal rights of the chicken.

After 1822, in the UK, some animal welfare legislation was passed that gave cattle, sheep and horses the legal right not to be treated cruelly. In time, similar laws were passed to protect other species, and certain kinds of entertainments – baiting animals, and organising fights between animals – were banned. In the UK and in some other countries, animals have some legal rights, but of a very limited scope.

Moral Rights

The law of your country defines what your legal rights are. Your legal rights will change if the law changes: before 1822, animals in the UK had no legal rights; afterwards they did.

There is a difference between the law as it is in a particular country, and the law as it should be. In many countries a few hundred years ago, slaves had no legal rights at all: a master could kill his slave if he wanted. We can criticise a law of a land because it is not as it should be; it does not recognise the *moral rights* of people in that country. You have a moral right if you have a claim that others *ought* to acknowledge. Slaves who had no legal rights nevertheless had a moral right not to be killed: a master who killed his slave was violating the slave's moral rights, even if no one could report him to a police force or have him punished by the law. Whereas it is fairly straightforward to tell what legal rights someone has – you find out what is forbidden and what permitted by the law – it is much harder to know what moral rights he or she has: you need to know what is *morally* permitted and forbidden.

If you have a right to something, you have a special claim to it, a claim that everyone must acknowledge. When you play cards, your opponent may have a very strong hand that would normally win the game; but if you have the trump card, it does not matter what other cards he or she has: victory is yours. A right is like a trump card: if you have a right, no matter how much anyone else would benefit from violating it, they must not do so. If you own your stereo, you have rights over it as your property: you are entitled to use it whenever you want, whether or not other people would enjoy it more than you do or play better music on it. Everyone else must acknowledge that you have the right over your own stereo and that you are entitled to refuse to give it up.

Suppose that there are five people dying in hospital with diseased organs. If the doctors painlessly killed you and distributed your healthy organs between the patients, they would all survive and lead happy and useful lives. Everyone else might be very much happier if the doctors chopped you up and shared out your organs. But you have a moral right to life, a trump card, which we must recognise. The rest of us might be better off if the doctors killed you, but your right means that we are not entitled to weigh up the benefits of your death against the costs to you: we must acknowledge that you are entitled to refuse to die.

You have moral status if it matters morally when you are harmed, but you can have this status without having any rights. If you had moral status, but no right to life, we would have to take into account the grave harm that we would do to you if we used your organs to save five other people's lives. But you would have no trump card: we would be entitled to weigh up the cost to you against the benefit to those five. If the benefit to the five were sufficiently great, it could be right to kill you for their sake. If you have moral status, what happens to you matters morally; but other things may matter even more.

Most people think that they have a right to life, that no one is entitled to kill them if they do not want to die, no matter how much everyone else might benefit from their death. But what if by killing someone, we could save millions of lives? Would it be wrong to sacrifice one human life to avert a terrible catastrophe? Many people think that in such extreme circumstances it would not be wrong to kill, even if the victim did not agree to die. So we do not think that anyone's right to life can trump the benefits of his or her death when those benefits are extraordinarily great. But in ordinary circumstances, each of us is entitled to refuse to be sacrificed: we humans have a right to life.

The Grounds of Moral Status

Since it is possible to have moral status without a right to life, we need to ask two separate questions about animals: do they have moral status? And do they have a right to life?

Why do we have moral status when sticks and stones do not? And is this crucial characteristic shared with animals? We have three features that might be the grounds of moral status.

First, we are members of a moral community. We recognise that other members of this community make moral claims on us just as we make moral claims on them, and we hold each other morally responsible for treating the others well. Second, we can feel pleasure and pain. And third, we are living creatures with needs. If our needs are not met, our lives will not be successful and eventually we will die.

In Chapters 7 and 8, we will assess whether animals have moral status by deciding which of these three is the ground of our moral status. Chapters 9 and 10 will address the question of the right to life.

CHAPTER SEVEN

THE MORAL COMMUNITY

In George Orwell's novel *Animal Farm*, a barnyard of animals, frustrated with the poor management of their drunken master Mr Jones, foment a revolution that drives out Jones and leaves them in charge of the farm. They come up with a set of seven rules to order their society, which they paint on the barn wall:

1. Whatever goes upon two legs is an enemy
2. Whatever goes upon four legs, or has wings, is a friend
3. No animal shall wear clothes
4. No animal shall sleep in a bed
5. No animal shall drink alcohol
6. No animal shall kill any other animal
7. All animals are equal

The animals accept these rules and live by them, until the leading pig Napoleon tightens his trotter-grip on power and their utopia unravels.

The creatures of *Animal Farm* are a moral community. They have formulated rules that award each other moral status, and, at least initially, they agree to stick to the rules. They have made a kind of contract together. This is remarkably similar to the way that many philosophers think humans gain moral status.

Ethics as a Contract

If a group of people lived together without any laws, their society would be chaotic. They would be in constant danger of harm from one another; their property would be stolen all the time. Their lives would be, in the words of Thomas Hobbes, 'nasty, brutish and short'. Any sensible people would get together to agree on a set of rules to make their lives safer and more orderly, just as the creatures of *Animal Farm* do.

Suppose that you and I live next to each other in the middle of nowhere, where there is no rule of law and no police force. We get together to decide on some rules. I don't want to be hurt, but I know that you could easily harm me and get away with it; after all, there's no police force to catch up with you. However, I also know that you don't want to be hurt either, and you know that I could easily harm you too. So I suggest that we make a deal: each person who signs up to the contract agrees that he or she has a reason not to harm the others, in return for their accepting that they have a reason not to harm him or her. Everyone who signs the contract now has moral status.

The theory that the rules of ethics are the rules that members of a society would agree to live by is called *contractualism*. Contractualists do not think that we have actually inscribed our signatures on a piece of paper agreeing to award each other moral status. Obviously we have not. They think that if we were rational and knew all the horrible consequences of not treating each other as having moral status, we would sign up.

In the real world, some people know that they are rich and strong. They can easily build a nice, big, gated apartment block to live in and protect themselves from the rest of society. They would have no need to sign up to a contract agreeing to treat anyone else as having moral status, because they know that they can protect themselves from murderers and thieves, and it may profit them in the future to treat other humans rather badly. In the real world, the most powerful members of a society might refuse to sign up to a contract agreeing to recognise other people's moral status.

But imagine that you were asked to sign a contract agreeing to the rules of your society without knowing what place you had in it, whether you were one of the rich and powerful or whether you were poor and weak. If the rules of your society did not include a rule to treat everyone as having moral status, and you were poor and weak, you would be at the mercy of the strong. You would live your whole life in fear and danger. Of course, you might turn out to be one of the powerful, and your life would go fine. But would you really want to take the risk? If you did not know what place you were going to have in a society, surely you should sign up to a set of rules that treated everyone, whether rich or poor, as having moral status.

In his book *A Theory of Justice*, John Rawls defended a version of contractualism. Imagine you are behind a 'veil of ignorance': you do not know what role you have in your society, and as a consequence you cannot choose rules that are biased towards yourself – you are forced to treat everyone fairly. Rawls thought that the rules agreed behind the veil of ignorance have a special authority: they are *the rules of justice*. According to Rawls, justice is only one part of ethics, for you morally ought to be kind and generous as well as just, so even though the rules of justice are defined by the contract, there may be important parts of ethics, including perhaps the parts that concern animals, which have nothing to do with contracts. By contrast, other contractualists, such as Peter Carruthers in his book *The Animals Issue*, think that the rules that you would choose behind the veil of ignorance are not merely the rules of justice, they are *the rules of all of morality*.

If the *whole* of ethics is defined by a contract, then whether you have moral status at all depends on whether you are part of the contract: you have moral status only because other people agree to take your interests into account, in return for your taking their interests into account. To participate in the contract you need to have two different qualities. First, you need to be able to assess different sets of rules and agree to a contract specifying the rules for your society. If you cannot imagine your society set up in different ways, with a rule against murder, or with no such rule, you cannot assess whether your society would be better with one set of rules rather than another and you cannot meaningfully choose one set over another.

Second, if you are going to persuade other people to take your interests into account, you need to assure them that you will act on the rules you both agreed rather than merely acting on your impulses or doing whatever you want. If you cannot help acting on violent antisocial impulses, other people are not going to allow you as part of their moral community and party to their contract. They will not see the point of agreeing to take your welfare into account, because however good your intentions, you are incapable of respecting their interests in return.

To be a member of a moral community, you need to be able to assess how you should treat others and to alter your behaviour on the basis of your assessment. Most humans can do both, and it is because of this that we hold them morally responsible for what they do. It is only morally responsible people who are part of a moral community, who can take part in contractual agreements. If ethical rules are the rules of a contract, only those who are morally responsible have moral status.

Are Animals Part of Our Moral Community?

According to contractualism about ethics, animals have moral status only if they are morally responsible for their actions. At the moment, we do not treat animals as part of our moral community; we do not treat them as capable of acknowledging the rules of our society, of taking our interests into account, or of having moral responsibility for what they do. But perhaps we are making a mistake.

Apes and some other animals that live in social groups seem to abide by a social code. For example, male chimps from the same social group will fight using their hands and feet but not their extremely dangerous teeth. These animals form a kind of primitive moral community, fitting their behaviour to the rules of their society. But they do not appear to be capable of reflecting on these rules, and assessing whether some other arrangement would be better. Since it is unlikely they could even grasp what it would be like to live under different laws, they cannot be said to give their consent to the rules by which they live.

When we house-train pets, we teach them a set of rules that they must obey; we call them naughty or good depending on how well they follow the rules, and punish them when they behave particularly badly. But these rules are not based on an agreement made between our pet and us. We do not expect pets to develop their own judgement about right and wrong and come to understand why they should accept the rules. Though many owners treat their pets like members of their own family, they still do not treat their pets as morally responsible.

In the past, however, some human societies did treat animals as part of their moral community. In various European countries between the 12th and 18th centuries, there were at least 93 criminal trials of animals. The animals were accused of a variety of crimes included killing children and bestiality (sexual intercourse between man and beast, both of whom were put on trial).

In France in 1379, three pigs that had trampled on the son of the swine-herd were condemned to death. The rest of the herd had hurried to the scene of the murder and were said to have grunted in approval of it. They were arrested as accomplices and sentenced to the same punishment.

In 1750 Jacques Ferron of Vanvres was found guilty of sexual intercourse with a she-ass and was sentenced to death. The animal was acquitted. It was judged that she was the victim of violence; she had been coerced into the act by Ferron and had not freely taken part in the crime.

These animals were given a full trial, usually in an ecclesiastic court, with lawyers for the prosecution and the defence just like in a human trial. If found guilty, the animals were punished with the same penalties that human criminals might expect, including hanging, burning and burying alive.

What was the purpose of animal trials? A pig might be treated as a scapegoat, and blamed even though everyone knew that it was not really guilty of a crime. But an animal trial was an expensive business; the lawyers for each side had to be paid. And the trial procedure was taken very seriously; animals were occasionally acquitted (as was the ass of Vanvres), and their cases could go to appeal. It is hard to see why anyone would bother with a full trial for an animal unless they thought that they were establishing whether or not the animal was genuinely responsible for a crime. On at least one occasion, a court considered this very

Treating animals as morally responsible: the execution of a sow

issue: the defence raised an objection to the trial on the basis that the animal defendants did not have the qualities, in particular the intelligence, to be responsible for a crime at all. But the defence was not accepted and the defendants were found guilty.

The people who put animals on trial apparently held these creatures morally responsible for their crimes, regarding animals as part of their moral community.

The very idea of putting animals in the dock seems ridiculous to us. We do not hold animals responsible because we do not think that they have the qualities needed for moral responsibility: they are not able to assess their reasons for action or evaluate moral rules; they act on instinct or on their desires, and cannot choose to act in the interests of others instead.

We cannot take it for granted that only humans have those qualities. Other animals too might be capable of autonomy; it might be appropriate to hold them morally responsible too. The people who tried animals seem to have thought that pigs and donkeys and even insects had those qualities. But our best understanding of animal minds is that those animals are not capable of autonomy, of assessing the reasons for an action and acting for the strongest reason, and so cannot be held responsible for what they do. Putting an animal on trial for a crime is a mistake, because animals simply cannot be guilty of a crime in the way that humans can.

Contractualism about the whole of ethics describes moral status as resting on participation in a moral community. Only those creatures that are morally responsible, that can agree to a set of social rules and modify their behaviour to fit with those rules, are part of the moral community and have moral status. If we discovered that some animals, perhaps the higher apes, were capable of making social agreements of the right kind with us, they would be part of our moral community and we would have to recognise their moral status. But as far as we know, no animals do have these qualities; none is autonomous, none can be a party to an ethical contract. Real animals, unlike the allegorical beasts Orwell describes in *Animal Farm*, are not morally responsible for what they do. So, according to contractualism about ethics, none has moral status.

Is the No Moral Status View Absurd?

According to contractualism about ethics, animals are more like sticks and stones than people. If we want to eat them, we can slaughter and cook them. If we want to hunt them, we can chase them and kill them. If we are interested in science, we can perform experiments on them. There are no limits to what we may do: it does not matter morally whether we kill them quickly or slowly, with suffering or without.

Do we treat animals as if they have no moral status? Many of us eat animals, use medicines that have been tested on them, and so on. But while we have no problem with many practices that harm animals, at the same time most of us think that there are some limits to what we may do to them. Cock-fighting, in which two birds fight to the death for the entertainment of a crowd, and bear-baiting, in which a bear is attacked by dogs, are both now considered wrong by most people, and are against the law. Many people think it is wrong to abandon or to mistreat your pets. But if animals have no moral status, there is absolutely nothing improper in abandoning Rover or Felix, and nothing amiss in encouraging animals to tear each other to pieces for our entertainment.

Contractualism about ethics is a *No Moral Status* view: it implies that animals do not matter morally. Most of us disagree. We think that it is unacceptable for us to treat animals with gratuitous cruelty; we should not torture an animal for our entertainment. Any theory that claims that there are no limits to what we may do to animals is surely ridiculously mistaken and we should reject it.

We should not be too hasty, however, in dismissing the view that animals lack moral status. Even if animals have no moral status, we have at least three kinds of reason to treat animals well: reasons of self-interest, as well as aesthetic and moral reasons.

Self-interest

Sometimes we benefit from treating animals well. We can train animals to do useful jobs; we can teach a dog to guard our house, or a cat to catch mice. It is difficult if not impossible to train a cat or a dog if you regularly fail to feed it properly or kick it and shout at it constantly. If you want to train an animal successfully, you have to treat it reasonably well. Furthermore, if you treat a cat or dog particularly badly, it may ultimately turn on you and attack you. So you have good reason not to treat the animals around you too badly.

Farmers have incentives to treat their animals fairly well too. If farm animals are kept in terrible conditions or fed too little of the wrong kind of food, they will not grow properly and may suffer from disease, cutting down the profits. Any sensible farmer will pay attention to the health of his or her animals.

If we care about our own interests, we have some reasons to treat animals well, but these reasons are few and are of no great importance. No one has a reason to refrain from doing anything they like to any animal that is incapable of attacking them or is of no use to them. If you are not interested in guard dogs or rat-catching cats, you have no reason to treat them well. And once a guard dog is too old to be helpful to you, you can do with it what you want. Anyone interested in eating animals should care about keeping the animals healthy and increasing their weight. But this will inevitably be balanced by other concerns, such as our interest in not spending too much money on our food. If it is too expensive to feed animals properly and keep them healthy, we may decide to eat inferior quality meat rather than to spend more money on farming.

Animals and Art

Think of a great work of art, like the statue of the *Venus de Milo*, or Van Gogh's paintings of sunflowers. Now imagine destroying it: taking a hammer and smashing the statue into tiny pieces, or ripping up the picture, setting light to it and turning it into a pile of ashes.

Many of us think that we ought not to destroy great works of art. But we do not think it is morally wrong to do so, for paintings and sculptures have no moral status. Instead they have aesthetic value: great paintings and sculptures are beautiful. We ought to appreciate beautiful things; if we destroy them, we make it impossible for us and for others to admire them. We have aesthetic reasons to treat works of art well; do we have aesthetic reasons to treat animals well too?

Some animals are beautiful. We can appreciate the elegance of a greyhound, the nobility of a stag, the colouring of a butterfly. Just as it would be wrong to destroy great works of art – the *Venus de Milo*, the paintings of Van Gogh – perhaps it would also be wrong to damage and destroy beautiful animals. In the same way that we must have failed to appreciate properly Van Gogh's *Sunflowers* were we to use it to light a fire, we must have failed to appreciate a stag properly were we to hunt it down and shoot it. Even if animals have no moral status, we may have reasons to treat at least some animals well, preserving the beauty of individual animals and making sure that species of attractive animals do not die out, so that they may be appreciated by future generations of humans.

We obviously do respond differently to animals that we find appealing than to those we find ugly or disgusting: many people who do not object to putting down rat-poison or killing cockroaches strongly disapprove of foxhunting and killing seals. It may be that we think that foxes and seals feel pain more keenly than cockroaches or rats. But it is more likely that we simply find attractive the bushy tail and intelligent face of the fox, the mournful eyes and sleek fur of the seal-pup, and sympathise with those animals when they suffer. By contrast, we find the yellow teeth and scaly tail of sewer-rats revolting, and as a consequence, we are wholly unmoved by their suffering and death. We feel more strongly that we ought to treat animals well when those animals are pretty.

We may have aesthetic reasons to treat some animals well, and it is likely that we do actually care more about animals we find attractive. But these reasons are extremely limited. We ought to appreciate beautiful animals but we have no aesthetic reason to treat well those animals we find ugly or repellent.

In any case, aesthetic reasons to treat animals well are reasons to preserve and enhance the attractiveness of beautiful animals. There is nothing wrong with treating them badly if we can do so without affecting their beauty. We have no aesthetic reason not to cause a fox considerable pain and suffering provided we could do so without damaging its appearance; in fact we have reason *not* to prevent its suffering if doing so would impair its attractiveness, for example, we have reason not to amputate an animal's painful limb if doing so would make that animal look less good. But surely the suffering we cause to an animal is far more important than what the animal looks like.

Indirect Moral Reasons

You might think that according to the No Moral Status view, we have no *moral* reasons to treat animals well. After all, isn't that what it means to deny that animals have moral status? But this is not quite right: if animals have no moral status, we can have no duties to protect an animal's interests for that creature's own sake. But we may have indirect duties to animals, duties that concern animals, but which are owed to other people.

The most obvious kind of indirect duty involves animals that are the property of other humans. If a farmer owns a barn, it would be against the law – and would be wrong – for you to damage or destroy it if the farmer does not want you to do so. Similarly, if a farmer owns a pig, you ought not to beat the pig or give it poison without his or her permission. There is, however, nothing wrong with harming an animal that you own, or whose owner has given you permission to go ahead. An animal can be treated in any way an owner pleases; other people must do what would be good in the judgement of the owner, not what would be good for the animal. And this of course offers no protection to foxes, deer and other wild animals that are not owned by anyone.

Many of us think that we have a moral reason not to treat any animal badly, whether or not it is anyone's property, and whether or not we have the owner's permission. Can someone who accepts the No Moral Status view agree?

Perhaps surprisingly, it seems that they can. Suppose that humans have moral status but animals do not. Now suppose that the way we treat animals affects how we treat humans – people who treat animals badly tend to treat humans badly too. If this is so, then it does after all matter morally how we treat animals.

Imagine that there is a gang of small boys who enjoy tormenting animals. They like to kick small dogs and cats, they try to set light to a cat's tail to see what will happen. It is not hard to guess what these boys will do as they get older: instead of targeting small animals that they can easily bully, they will turn to weak and vulnerable people, smaller children, the elderly, stealing from them and tormenting them as much as they can.

These boys enjoy causing pain to animals, making them suffer for their own amusement. According to the No Moral Status view, their treatment of animals is not bad in itself, but it is bad because in hurting animals for no good reason, the boys become cruel. As they get older, they act cruelly towards other humans, not just towards animals. Their earlier treatment of animals is wrong because it leads them to go on to treat humans – who have moral status – dreadfully.

But is it really true that *everyone* who makes animals suffer for trivial reasons will go on to do the same to humans? After all, anyone who accepts a No Moral Status view of animals thinks that there is a huge difference between causing humans to suffer and causing animals to suffer: in one case you are harming creatures with a moral status, in the other, you are not. In one case, causing harm matters morally, in the other case, it does not. This will surely affect whether you progress from hurting animals to hurting people. If the gang of young boys torment animals for fun but do not go on to torment humans – perhaps because they accept a No Moral Status view – there is nothing wrong with what they do according to that theory.

In fact, there may be some people who are *less* likely to hurt humans if they harm animals. Some people may take out their frustration at people – their families, their colleagues at work – on animals. Instead of hitting their boss, they may come home and kick the cat or yell at the dog. If you are one of these people, if kicking the cat makes you less likely to kick a human, then hurting the cat is not wrong, according to the No Moral Status view. In fact, it might even be your *duty* to take out your aggression on a creature with no moral status, instead of a human whose suffering matters morally.

If you treat animals cruelly are you more likely to go on to be cruel to humans? This is really a question of psychology that can be answered only through careful observation of those who harm animals. But there are several reasons why we might expect there to be a link between violence towards animals and violence towards people. If you often express your anger through violent action, you may find it hard to control your aggression or express it in a different way. If you enjoy acting violently, you may find it hard to stop yourself doing so at every opportunity, whether against humans, animals or inanimate objects.

But if this is right, you should try to control your anger in all circumstances, whether it is directed at sticks and stones, animals or humans – it ought to be as bad to kick a rock as it is to kick a cat – which is obviously absurd.

But this does not take into account the extra link between

violence to animals and violence to people. Unlike rocks and other inanimate objects, animals feel pain. If you kick the cat, it hurts the cat; a rock doesn't suffer no matter what you do to it. Violence towards animals is much more similar to violence towards humans than anything you might do to a rock. Kicking Felix the cat is more likely to lead you to kick people, because in both cases you relieve your frustration by causing pain to others.

But as soon as we admit that violence to animals and violence to people is quite similar, we should question the No Moral Status view. According to that theory, people have a moral status and how we treat them matters morally; animals have no moral status. But people and animals are actually very similar. Doesn't the fact that they both feel pain mean that it matters morally how we treat them both? Just as we should not cause people to suffer unnecessarily, isn't it also true that we should not cause animals to suffer unnecessarily, for the sake of the animals themselves, not only for the sake of people? If it is in fact true that small boys who are cruel to animals become cruel to people, perhaps it is because they recognise that *morally*, causing pain to humans is very similar to causing pain to animals. They know that *both* matter morally: they simply do not care.

It is hard to see how, if human pain matters morally, animal pain could not. But if it matters morally when you cause pain to animals, then animals that can feel pain must have moral status.

Contractualism about the whole of ethics makes moral status depend on whether a creature is morally responsible, part of a moral community; since animals are not part of the moral community, they have no moral status. According to this theory, it is sometimes wrong to treat these animals badly, because we have self-interested, aesthetic and indirect moral reasons to treat them well. But it cannot take account of our *direct* moral reasons not to make animals suffer pain *for their own sake.* Since animals that can feel pain do matter morally, we have to reject contractualism about ethics, and reject the idea that moral status depends on being part of a moral community.

CHAPTER EIGHT

PAIN, PLEASURE AND THE VALUE OF LIFE

Imagine that on a very cold day the pavements have become icy. An old lady has slipped over and is lying on the floor. A crowd have gathered round her, but instead of helping her up and making sure she is not hurt, they are laughing at her. One of them amuses his friends by pushing over other elderly people. The crowd find this hilarious.

The elderly people who are laughed at by the crowd have bruises and broken bones. They are frightened by what is happening to them. They suffer from physical pain, shock and fear.

No reasonable person could deny that the behaviour of this crowd is disgusting. They ought to be trying to help the vulnerable; instead they enjoy these people's suffering and encourage the particularly appalling individual who goes round pushing people over. The crowd are cruel; it is wrong to find these people's pain amusing.

Now imagine that a dog is chained up to a lamppost. It has been left without food and water and is now very weak. A crowd has gathered round the dog. Two members of the crowd are teasing the dog by throwing stones at it. Whenever one of them throws a stone, the dog tries to attack them, but is held back by its chain. After a time, it stops trying to fight back and starts trying to avoid being hit. The crowd encourages the stone-throwers until the dog refuses to respond; then they get bored and leave.

This group of people is cruel and callous in exactly the same way as the first crowd, enjoying watching another creature's pain and fear. They should have tried to make sure the dog was not hurt; they certainly should not have encouraged people to harm the dog even more.

Of course, there are important differences between humans and the animals that can feel pain. We humans can *anticipate* pain; the elderly people walking down the street could see what was happening to the others and naturally they worried that the same might happen to them, that they too might be pushed over and ridiculed. We can *imagine* different scenarios too: the people who were trapped on the pavement could picture the crowd stealing from them, kicking them or even killing them. Even if it is unlikely that the crowd would ever kill their victims and they never actually do, the thought of what *might* happen to them makes what actually occurs seem even worse. We can also *remember* what has happened to us. Every time one of the people left stranded on the ground recalled their ordeal they would feel a shiver of fear: they would continue to suffer even after the events were over.

Some animals may be able to anticipate what may happen to them in the future; some may be capable of imagining different scenarios; some may be able to remember what happened to them in the past. But most animals do not have these capacities to the same extent as humans, and it is likely that there are animals that can feel pain but have no imagination and no capacity for anticipating or remembering harm. Suppose that a human and a cow are both hit with a stick. We might at first think that this causes each of them the same amount of pain, but in fact the human may suffer more than the cow because the human will anticipate feeling the pain and will be able to imagine much worse beatings that might be inflicted, whereas the cow will not. There are important differences between the capacities for suffering of creatures that have imagination and memory, and creatures that do not.

Animals that can feel pain but cannot anticipate or remember their own distress can nevertheless suffer. Painful and frightening sensations are bad whoever experiences them, whether human or animal. It matters morally what we do to animals that can feel pain: we ought not to cause them pain unnecessarily, without good reason. Since their suffering matters morally, animals that can feel pain must have moral status.

Though many animals can suffer, as we saw in Chapter 3, all plants, and probably some animals, can experience nothing at all. Does it matter morally what happens to these: are they mere objects, or do they have moral status?

We humans feel pain and pleasure, we prefer that some things happen to us and that some do not, and we value certain things in our lives. There is a very straightforward sense in which we can say that something is good or bad for us from our own perspective. It is unlikely that any non-human creatures value what happens to them; as far as we know, no other animals can assess their lives as good or bad. Some animals may have desires, perhaps for food, water and shelter. But even if a creature has no desires but merely acts on instincts, provided that it has positive and negative experiences, we can make sense of what is good and bad for it from its own point of view, even if it could not possibly describe things in that way itself: we can say that something is bad for the creature from its own perspective if it causes the creature pain, and is good for it in its own eyes if it causes pleasure. A sentient creature has moral status, because some things matter from its own point of view, and what matters to it should matter to us.

Plants have no values, no preferences and no experiences at all. Since no plant has a point of view, nothing that happens to it – whether it gets plenty of sun and nutrients and grows to be enormous or is chopped up for firewood – matters to it. Similarly, nothing that happens to an insentient single-celled bacterium can matter from its own perspective.

Many people argue that only those creatures that can suffer have moral status, because they think that harm matters morally only if it matters from the point of view of that which is harmed. Environmentalists disagree. They argue that plants and non-sentient animals have moral status too, even though they cannot feel pain or pleasure, simply because they are alive. They claim that we should not harm any living thing without good reason: we should have a reverence for life.

Reverence for Life

I put weed-killer down in my garden to kill off dandelions and thistles so that my lawn looks good in the summer.

I go away on holiday and forget about my houseplant. It gradually shrivels up. When I return from holiday, I try to revive it with lots of water but it's too late. The plant dies.

The tree at the end of my garden has grown much taller in the last few years and is now blocking out the light. I cut down the tree to let in more light, so I can sit outside eating breakfast in the sun.

Have I done wrong?

You and I can thrive or our lives can go badly. Our lives go well if we are healthy, well fed and happy; badly when we are ill, poor, hungry and in pain. For our lives to go well, we need certain things: we have basic needs for food, shelter, water in order to live at all, and we need other things – free speech, some education, some money – to lead a really good life.

It is often thought that we have moral rights for the kinds of things that are basic needs for us: we have a right to life, for example, because it is impossible to have a good life if we are killed or are in constant danger from murderers. But the relationship between needs and rights is controversial. I need food and water to survive: does this mean that I have a right that you give me food and water if I will die without it? What if you own the food and refuse to give it up – aren't you entitled to do what you want with your own property? What if we both need food to survive, but there is only enough for one of us – do we both have a right over the same piece of bread? My right may not automatically follow from my need, for you may have competing needs, and maybe competing rights too, that should be taken into account. But even if we leave aside the difficult question of rights, we might think that our moral status depends on our having lives that can go well or badly, and our having needs that must be met if we are to flourish.

Animals' lives can go well or badly too. A dog or a cow needs food, water, a certain kind of environment, otherwise it will become ill and die. If the moral status of humans depends on the fact that our lives can go well or badly and that we have basic needs, then animals would have moral status too, as they also have basic needs that must be met if they are to flourish. Even animals like invertebrates that perhaps cannot feel pain or pleasure need the right kind of environment in order to live at all, so these too would have moral status.

As well as humans and animals, however, plants can flourish or do badly. Plants have basic needs; they thrive when they are grown in the right kind of soil, when they have access to nutrients, water and sunlight. If they are in the wrong kind of environment, they will not develop properly and eventually will die. If moral status did depend on whether something could flourish or do badly, plants would have moral status too.

Environmentalists think that killing plants and animals can be morally wrong, just as killing humans is wrong. They claim that it is wrong to kill weeds just to make your lawn look nicer. It is wrong to let your houseplants die of neglect. And it is wrong to cut down a tree so that you can eat breakfast outdoors. Are they correct: do trees, houseplants and weeds have moral status?

Our Place in the Web of Life

Environmentalists think that we are arrogant and foolish to see our environment as something that we can use in any way we choose. We ought to appreciate that plants, animals and people are all part of a web of life that is fragile and easily destroyed. If we damage part of the web, we cannot expect the rest of it to stay the same. We cannot isolate ourselves and remain unaffected. We depend on it for our survival; in threatening plants, we are threatening ourselves.

As a consequence, environmentalists argue, we need to change the way we treat living creatures. We have to recognise that plants and animals are not our tools, we must be less egotistic about our own importance in the web of life, and wiser in understanding how much we depend on our environment.

We might interpret this environmentalist argument as giving us *self-interested* reasons for tending to our environment and looking after plants and animals. After all, since we rely on the environment, we would be very foolish to risk damaging it so badly that it no longer provided air for us to breathe and clean water for us to drink. But significant environmental damage is often very slow. We have a very strong reason not to set off a nuclear bomb that would

115

immediately contaminate the world and which would certainly affect us, but we have much less powerful reasons to give up the slow poisoning of the world's atmosphere, rivers and lakes with industrial pollution, for we will be long dead by the time this will have an effect.

On the other hand, if we pollute the planet, our grandchildren will have no clean air or water. If we care about what happens to them – and we should, because they will be persons with moral status just like us – we should change our ways. We should try to leave the world safe for them.

This environmentalist argument appeals to our own interests and the interests of future generations of humans. We could accept this argument even while thinking that plants have no moral status. We have good reasons to care about the environment for the sake of humans, even if we are indifferent to plants for their own sake. But though environmentalists certainly impress on us how much our future welfare and the welfare of our grandchildren depend on our environment, their view is *not* that we should protect our community of life for the sake of some privileged members of it, the humans; instead, we should protect it for the sake of *all* its members, human, plant or animal. The living plants and animals in our environment are not tools to help humans survive, but are valuable for their own sake, and as part of a valuable ecosystem.

Suppose that there is a complex ecosystem made up of trees, shrubs, wild flowers and ferns, but no animals. These plants are rare and beautiful. The ecosystem has survived in a similar form for thousands of years, and would probably survive for thousands more if no one intervened. If that web of life is worth preserving, it must be because the plants it contains are valuable; its value cannot depend on the moral status of animals or humans, for no animals or humans are part of it.

Imagine that you found such an ecosystem on a lonely planet in a distant galaxy that you and your team of astronauts are visiting. You know that no other humans will probably ever visit this planet. You could blast off in your shuttle from the ecosystem, setting light to the plants with your booster rockets and destroying them, or you could leave from the other side of the planet, a deserted wasteland in which nothing grows. Surely you should set off from the deserted part of the planet rather than destroying all the plants. And surely you ought to do this because the plants themselves are morally valuable?

Not necessarily. The plants of this ecosystem may have no moral status, but some other kind of value. Some of the plants are beautiful. The complex interconnections between the different living organisms are intricate and elegant. It may be true that you ought not to destroy the ecosystem, but for aesthetic rather than moral reasons.

When Does an Organism Flourish?

Suppose that the environmentalists are right that plants and animals do have moral status because they are living things that can flourish or do badly. In that case, there must be a set of standards that should be used to judge whether a particular plant or animal is flourishing. But what could these standards be?

If we are dealing with animals that have preferences or that can feel pleasure and pain, we know that things can be good or bad for those animals from their own perspective. But how should we judge whether plants are doing well? It is true that plants and animals can thrive or do badly, they can live for longer, grow larger, avoid disease, and successfully reproduce. But it is not always straightforward to judge when an organism is flourishing. Usually, it is better for a plant to grow bigger: larger plants tend to be thriving better than smaller plants. But there would be something wrong with a dwarf rose that grew too large; it would not be a good specimen of that type of plant. Is a large dwarf rose thriving or not? If we judge the plant as a rose, it is; if we judge it as a dwarf variety, it is not.

Bulldogs are bred so that their faces are flat and squashed; this makes it difficult for them to breathe. Is a bulldog whose face is not squashed flourishing or not? In one sense it is thriving, for it can breathe freely; in another sense it is not, because it lacks one of the characteristic features of a good bulldog. There are no 'natural' standards for judging a bulldog or a dwarf rose: what could possibly decide which standards we ought to use? We have to choose a set of standards to judge how well a plant or animal is doing, depending on why we *want* to make the assessment. If we are interested in whether a dog can breathe easily, we will make one kind of assessment; if we are interested in pedigree bulldogs, we will make another. It is never true that a plant should *really* be judged as a dwarf variety: it is up to us.

Think of a chicken, bred to live in a factory farm from a long line of factory-farmed birds. It is characteristic of a factory-farmed chicken to live a short life in extremely cramped conditions. If we judge how well this chicken is thriving by the standards of other battery birds, it is flourishing. Of course, compared with free-range birds, it is unhealthy, has a poor diet and cannot move around properly: in that sense, it is not thriving at all. It makes a huge difference whether we compare our chicken with free-range birds or with other battery-farmed birds. But which comparisons ought we to make? If it is up to us which standards to use, we have no means of deciding whether factory-farmed birds are really thriving or not. Of course, we can try to work out whether factory-farmed birds suffer more than free-range birds, but then we would have given up on the task of trying to decide whether the animals are flourishing or not, relative to some set of standards. Instead we would be trying to find out whether they are doing well or badly from their own perspective. In other words, we would be taking sentience, not having basic needs, as the basis for moral status.

Sentience as the Ground of Moral Status

If plants had moral status, it would be as bad to harm plants as to kill and eat animals. Most of what we do every day would be wrong, for we kill carrots, leeks, potatoes and other plants all the time. It is unlikely that we could find enough food without eating either plants or animals. If plants and animals had equal moral status we would inevitably do wrong just by eating enough to survive.

If plants had moral status, much of our current agricultural practices and our everyday gardening would be wrong too: it would be immoral to kill thistles and dandelions, to get rid of a plant you did not like any more, to move a plant to a less suitable soil because you wanted a plant of a certain colour in that area of the garden, or to cut down a tree because it was blocking your light.

A moral theory that claimed that plants had moral status would be ridiculously demanding. We would have to think about how our actions affected plants as well as animals, and we would almost be guaranteed to act wrongly much of the time. The consequences of such a theory are absurd: ordinary weeding in the garden is obviously not immoral.

Some environmentalists believe that all life is morally valuable, and that we should have reverence for every living creature. But this is an extreme view: it would mean that ordinary farming and ordinary gardening were morally wrong, and it would be improper of us to kill plants, even if we needed to do so to survive. These environmentalists must also be committed to the claim that there is some set of standards we ought to use to judge whether a plant or animal is flourishing, though in fact it seems that there are many different standards that we could legitimately use, depending on why we want to make the assessment. The balance of reasons is against accepting the environmentalists' view that we should have reverence for all life. Instead we should accept that, since nothing can matter from the perspective of a living organism that cannot experience pleasure or pain, what happens to it does not matter morally. Only creatures that can feel pleasure and pain have moral status.

CHAPTER NINE

THE RIGHT TO LIFE

In 1993, Peter Singer and Paola Cavalieri founded the Great Ape Project. They and other animal rights activists began a campaign for an improvement in the treatment of the animals most closely related to us. Their goals were set out in a document they called *A Declaration on Great Apes*:

> We demand the extension of the community of equals to include all great apes: human beings, chimpanzees, bonobos, gorillas and orang-utans.

> The community of equals is the moral community within which we accept certain basic moral principles or rights as governing our relations with each other and enforceable at law. Among these principles or rights are the following:
> 1. The Right to Life
> 2. The Protection of Individual Liberty
> 3. The Prohibition of Torture

In the last few chapters, we have acknowledged that animals that can suffer have moral status. But the *Declaration on Great Apes* goes well beyond this. It holds that we should accept the great apes as part of our moral community. We have already seen reason to doubt this, for it is unlikely that any animals, even the great apes, are autonomous, and hence they are not morally responsible for their actions, which is a condition of participation in a moral community.

The *Declaration* adds that scientific experimentation on the great apes should be prohibited as a form of torture, and that they ought never to be killed except in self-defence. It claims that the great apes have rights.

As we saw in Chapter 6, having a right is like having a trump card that overrides whatever cards other people are holding. It means that other people are not entitled to do certain things to you, however much doing so would be in their interests. If you have a right to life, no one is entitled to kill you even if they would thereby inherit a fortune and everyone else would be glad you were out of the way. If an animal had a right to life, no one should kill and eat it; no one should hunt it; no one should infect it with deadly diseases for the benefit of mankind.

Many animal welfare campaigners believe that many animals, not just the great apes, have the right to life. But some sceptics think that it makes no sense to award animals rights, even if they have moral status. Why do they think that animal rights are absurd?

Rights and Responsibilities

It is a common saying that you cannot have rights unless you have responsibilities too. Some philosophers have turned this into an argument against animal rights. Since animals are not autonomous and cannot acknowledge the rights of humans or other animals, no animal can have responsibilities; so, these philosophers claim, no animal can have rights. In fact, they continue, it would be unfair to treat animals as if they had rights, because you would have to treat them as if they had responsibilities, and punish them for killing or harming other animals. It would obviously be ridiculous to send a fox to jail for attacking a chicken; it is equally ridiculous to claim that the fox – or the chicken – has rights. Or so says the hunt-loving philosopher Roger Scruton, in his book *Animal Rights and Wrongs*:

> A creature with rights is duty-bound to respect the rights of others. The fox would be duty-bound to respect the right to life of the chicken and whole species would be condemned out of hand as criminal by nature … any morality which *really* attributed rights to animals would constitute a gross and callous abuse of them.

We saw in Chapter 5 that we have no evidence that animals can reflect on their reasons for action and choose to act on what they think are good reasons. As a consequence, it is indeed a mistake to hold animals responsible for what they do. Foxes cannot be duty-bound to respect the rights of chickens; no animal can acknowledge the rights of anyone or anything. It would be totally inappropriate to punish animals for what they do naturally when they could not choose to do otherwise.

Scruton is correct that animals have no responsibilities. Does it follow that they have no rights?

There is an important sense in which rights and responsibilities do go together. If Alistair makes a promise to Ben, Ben has a right that Alistair keeps his promise, and Alistair has a responsibility to do so. If Charlie has the right to life, then Alistair, Ben and everyone else have a duty not to kill him.

Rights and responsibilities always come in pairs, but notice that it is not always the same person who has both the right and the responsibility. *Charlie's* right to life goes together with a duty on *everyone else* not to kill him. *Ben's* right depends on *Alistair's* responsibility. Though it is true that there cannot be a right without a responsibility, the right can be mine, the responsibility yours.

Suppose that animals have a right to life. Then all of us have a duty not to kill them, just as Charlie's right to life means that we all have a duty not to kill him. Nothing need follow about what responsibilities Charlie has, nor what responsibilities animals have: they may have many duties, or none at all. Scruton is mistaken: animals can have rights without themselves having any responsibilities.

Scruton might accept this argument, but reply that when we look closely into the origin of our rights, we will find that only those who have responsibilities actually do have rights. In particular, if rights depended on a kind of contract, no one could have rights without responsibilities. In Chapter 7, we argued that moral status is not based on any such agreement: perhaps moral status does not depend on a contract, but rights do.

Suppose that as before, you and I live next to each other in the middle of nowhere without a police force. Again, we get together to decide on some rules to live by. This time, we do not just award each other moral status. If I have moral status, you will not harm me unless you have very good reason to do so, but we both know that there might be circumstances where you do have good reason to kill me: perhaps you would benefit enormously by consolidating our two farms. Similarly, there might be circumstances where I have good reason to kill you. Even if we both acknowledge the other's moral status, we are not guaranteed to be safe from each other. Since both of us are very keen not to die, we reach an arrangement: we will each accept that the other has not just moral status, but a right to life. Each of us agrees to acknowledge a duty not to kill the other that overrides other reasons we might have to do so.

Now each of us has a right to life, because each of us has a duty not to kill the other. We acquired our rights and duties at exactly the same time when we made our joint agreement.

If we acquired our rights and duties by a kind of social contract, it would be impossible to have rights without responsibilities. Why would I agree to acknowledge that anyone has a right to life, that I have a duty not to kill them, unless they recognised my right to life in return? I have no reason to take on a duty not to kill animals because they will never pay me the compliment of recognising my rights.

This argument that animals have no rights rests on the claim that all rights depend on a social contract or agreement. But we seem to attribute rights to some humans – to babies, to the mentally disabled – who cannot acknowledge our rights. We cannot rule out the possibility that there are humans who have rights without responsibilities; so we ought to accept at least the possibility that animals might have no duties but nevertheless have rights. Whether they in fact have any particular right without any corresponding responsibilities depends on the basis of that individual right.

The Rights of Predators and Their Prey

Animals might have rights even though they have no responsibilities. But perhaps in fact it is impossible for all animals to have the right to life. If chickens have a right to life, don't we have a duty to save chickens by stopping foxes from attacking them? In fact, don't we have a duty to save any prey from its predators?

The idea that we might have such a duty is simply absurd, say those who reject animal rights. For one thing, the duty would be immensely demanding. We would have to be constantly policing the natural world, leaping in as a predator closed down on its defenceless victim. We would have no time for anything else; and no acceptable moral theory would tell us to spend all our time supervising nature.

But worse, it might make no sense for all animals to have the right to life. Suppose we succeeded in preventing all foxes from attacking chickens. Foxes would get food only when they came across a chicken or some other animal that had died of natural causes. Most foxes would not find enough food and would starve to death. If we protect prey from its predator, we are in danger of preventing the predator from getting a decent meal, and ultimately violating its right to life too. It is not possible for all animals to have a right to life because it would be impossible for anyone to respect the rights of predators *and* the rights of their prey. So animals do not have the right to life.

This argument depends on what it means to have the right to life. If a chicken has the right to life, does that mean that I have to protect it from any harm that might befall it, ensuring that it stays alive as long as possible? Or does it merely mean that I myself must not wring its neck? If a fox has the right to life, does it follow that I have to make sure that it gets enough to eat so that it stays alive as long as possible? Or is it just that I must not hunt it or shoot it?

Some philosophers have questioned whether there is any important distinction between killing someone and failing to protect them from dying: since it is bad for chickens to be killed and eaten, surely it must be just as bad for them to be eaten by a fox as to be eaten by me. If it is wrong for me to kill and eat the chicken myself, how can it be right for me to let the fox kill and eat it, when I could stop this happening?

On the other hand, many people who think humans have the right to life believe that though we have a duty not to kill, we do not have such a stringent duty to protect other people from dying. After all, everyone must die eventually: we simply could not protect people from death for ever. Many people think that we are not required to keep people alive for as long as we can by whatever means possible – it may sometimes be acceptable to choose not to resuscitate someone who is very ill from a terminal disease and suffering great pain – but it is not acceptable to kill them. It is worse to stab or strangle a person than to fail to send money to charity, even when that charity saves people's lives. When we attribute the right to life to humans, we mean that we have a duty not to kill, not a duty to protect them from death. When we attribute the right to life to animals, we should mean the same thing: we must not kill animals but need not protect them from their predators. If the right to life is defined in this way, no absurd consequences need follow: I must not kill chickens for food or hunt foxes, but I am required neither to protect the chicken from the fox nor to make sure that the fox does not starve. I can respect the rights of predators and prey without being constantly in demand as nature's policeman.

It is not absurd to attribute rights to animals. Since we ought not to cause animals pain for no good reason, we should acknowledge that animals have at least one right, the right that their suffering is taken into account.

But those who defend animal rights claim that some animals at least have many more rights than this: in particular, animals have a right not to be eaten for food, a right not to be hunted and a right not to be the subject of scientific experimentation. We think that humans have these rights because humans have a right to life. What is the basis of this right: why is it wrong to kill humans? There may be several reasons, but the most obvious is that it is wrong to kill humans because their death is bad.

Why Is Death Bad?

There are lots of reasons why death is bad. Death can be particularly terrible not just for the person who dies but for those who are still alive. When you die you leave behind many people, your friends, family and colleagues, who miss you. Your colleagues feel sad, while your husband or wife, children or parents are devastated. Some people are missed more than others. Some people have no one to grieve for them when they die; but their death is still bad.

Before you are dead, you go through a process of dying which can be deeply unpleasant. A prolonged, undignified and painful death is much worse than one that is swift and painless. But a premature death is bad even if it is quick and without pain.

Why is this so? After all, once you die, surely nothing matters to you any more. A throbbing headache is bad for you because it feels painful and unpleasant. But once you are dead, you cannot suffer pain at all. Losing a leg is bad for you because you are constantly frustrated in your attempts to do many of the things you want: you cannot walk down to the shops or run for the bus any more, your dream of becoming a professional footballer will never come true. But once you are dead you have no desires. You have no frustrations: there is nothing you dream about or hope to achieve.

Death is bad precisely *because* you do not experience anything, want anything or dream of anything when you are dead. After your death you will never have any more pleasure, successful projects or valuable relationships. Once you are dead you can no longer satisfy many of the desires you had when alive: a premature death prevents you from becoming a footballer just as surely as does losing a leg. Death is bad because you can no longer have any of these goods. If you had lived for longer, you could have achieved greater things and enjoyed yourself more.

Of course everyone must die at some time and some people are deprived of more when they die. If a toddler James dies in an accident when he would otherwise have lived for another 80 years, his death is particularly bad because he misses out on so many good things. If Sarah dies in her sleep at the age of 95 after a long, full and happy life, her death is not so bad for her. She would not have expected to enjoy a much longer life even if she had not died when she did. When we judge how bad a death is, we ought to take into account how much more life a person could reasonably have expected to enjoy if he or she had not died prematurely, and what quality of life he or she would have had. Suppose that Jeremy has cancer. He has no chance of recovery and could only expect to suffer unbearable pain in the remainder of his life. He is not deprived of much when he dies; in fact, death may be a welcome release for him.

The Deaths of Humans and the Deaths of Animals

How bad is it for an animal to die? Dying can be bad for animals just as it is for humans: an animal may suffer terribly from a long and painful process of dying, though most animals would not experience the indignities associated with severe illness in the way that we do.

Some animals seem to understand what it means for other animals to die, and there are anecdotes of elephants that appear to mourn their dead. But many animals do not understand what death is; many animals are not upset for the death of one of their number, even of a creature closely related to them. The death of a human is often worse than the death of an animal for those who are left behind.

Suppose that an animal dies quickly and painlessly and no other creatures realise it is dead and mourn it. Is its death bad? When an animal dies, it misses out on the pleasures it would have experienced if it had lived for longer; its death is bad because it is deprived of these goods. If the animal were young and healthy, it would be deprived of many pleasant experiences; if it were very sick, it would not have had much of a life even if it had lived for longer, and its death would not be as bad.

The deaths of humans and animals are bad for similar reasons: in each case, the victim is deprived of what they would have enjoyed had they lived longer. To compare the deaths of humans and animals, we need to compare the kinds of goods humans and animals would typically have experienced if they had not died. Of course, the death of each human and each animal will be different. Some deaths are a welcome release, when the human or animal would only have suffered if they had lived for longer. Some deaths are not very bad, because the human or animal would not have enjoyed many goods in the rest of the life they would have had. But would a human who died prematurely *typically* miss out on more or less than an animal that died young?

Animals are capable of simple pleasures, of eating, drinking, finding a mate and so on; these are the things they are deprived of by death. Humans enjoy these simple pleasures too. But human life is much more complicated than animal life, and there are many kinds of pleasure that humans can enjoy but animals cannot. We enjoy reading philosophy and poetry, listening to music, watching films, making works of art and appreciating what other artists have produced. The philosopher John Stuart Mill (1806–73) thought that 'higher' pleasures like the pleasures of art were more valuable than the 'lower' pleasures of which animals are capable. Perhaps it is true that if they had the choice, most humans would prefer to enjoy higher pleasures at least some of the time; we would find an animal life of simple pleasures unsatisfying. But whether or not some kinds of pleasure are more valuable than others, it is certainly true that humans can take pleasure in a much greater variety of activities than can animals, and so are deprived of more by an early death.

Some of our most precious pleasures come from spending time with our friends and family. An early death cuts these relationships short, before they can develop fully. Many animals, even those that live in social groups, do not have friendships with other creatures that are intimate and enduring and that mature in the way that human relationships can. Animals cannot be deprived of such relationships by a premature death; but humans can.

Most of us make plans and projects for our life. We want to have a successful career; we want to see our children grow up healthy and happy. An early death prevents us from carrying out our plans and seeing our projects come to fruition; it frustrates all our hopes for the future. Many animals have no concept of the future and cannot think about it at all; they certainly have no projects they would like to carry out in their later life that would be frustrated when they died. Some animals may be able to think of themselves, and they may have a few simple plans: they may hope to have a mate and plenty of food. But they certainly have no projects as complex as ours, and they have many fewer preferences for the future that would be thwarted by a premature death.

As well as planning for the future, many of us try to make sense of our lives as a complex whole; our capacity to see events as contributing to that whole can significantly alter their value for us. Something bad that happens to you when you are young can be *redeemed* if it contributes to something good that happens to you later on. The misery of your early life is not so bad if you can learn not to make the same mistake with your own children. The struggle of passing exams as a student becomes worthwhile when you succeed in your career. If you die before you enjoy success in your life, any early mistakes you made, any unhappiness you suffered cannot be redeemed. Most animals cannot reflect on their life as a whole, and most cannot devise or carry out projects sufficiently complex so that early incidents can contribute to a project that is good overall. The suffering of animals cannot be redeemed, however long the animal lives; an early death could not deprive them of this benefit.

It is usually bad for a human or an animal to die early, because they miss out on many good things that they would have enjoyed if they had lived for longer. Arguably, the goods that humans can enjoy are more valuable than the goods that animals can enjoy. But in any case, it is certainly true that humans miss out on a much greater variety of good things when they die than do animals and they have many more complex plans and projects that are frustrated.

It is also true that the deaths of some animals are likely to be worse than the deaths of others. The more sophisticated an animal's mind, the wider the range of goods it can experience: it will be able to pursue a greater variety of more complex projects, it may be able to form more sophisticated emotional bonds with other creatures, and it may even have some concept of itself and its own life. Death is likely to be worse for the more intellectually developed animals, including the higher apes, than it is for other creatures, just as usually the early death of a human will be worse than the early death of an animal.

What's Wrong with Killing?

It is natural to think that it is wrong to kill any human, because death is bad for each of them. It is certainly true that killing humans causes their death and their deaths are typically bad. But in fact, as we have seen, death is worse for some humans than for others. It is worse for the toddler James to die when he would otherwise have enjoyed many happy years than for the nonagenarian Sarah who would have died soon afterwards anyway. But it is morally wrong to kill Sarah, just as it is morally wrong to kill James.

All normal humans have the right to life; it is wrong to kill any of them, even though death is much worse for some than for others. Their right to life must be based in part on the fact that death is bad for them, but at least in part on something else that they all have to the same extent.

Normal humans can consent or object to what happens to them in their lives. They can assess whether they think that there are good reasons for them to die – for example perhaps their organs could be used to save the lives of several other people – and choose whether or not to die for those reasons. We ought to respect people's own decisions about their life, whether or not we are inclined to agree with their judgement, especially when those decisions are about something as important as their own death and even more so when what we are proposing is bad for them. It is wrong to do something harmful to a person, such as to take one of their organs for transplant, when they have withheld their consent and asked us not to go ahead, and it is wrong to do so without bothering to ask for their consent. In both cases, we would be refusing to take account of the victim's judgements about their own life; we would be denying that their decisions matter.

Murder is wrong because death is bad and because

typically people do not consent to be killed. Because we should respect a human's choice about their own life, each has the right to prevent us from doing harmful things to them, even if we would thereby benefit a great deal. This is a person's 'trump card', their right to life. A person is entitled to refuse to die for the sake of others.

As far as we know, no non-human animals can give or withhold their consent to anything. They cannot understand any complex situation, and they cannot assess whether or not there are good reasons for them to live or die.

Animal rights activists argue that we should never kill humans without consent, and since animals cannot give their consent, we should never kill animals either; so animals have a right to life. They claim that we deny animals a right to life to protect our own interests, because we benefit so much from killing them.

This argument is fundamentally mistaken. It is wrong to kill a person without their consent because we should respect a person's judgement about their own life, especially when we are proposing to do something as harmful to them as killing them. But animals cannot make judgements about their own life. They cannot meaningfully give their consent or withhold it. If we do something to them without their consent, we are not failing to respect their own assessment of what to do with their life because they cannot make that assessment.

If some animal were to have the capacity meaningfully to give its consent to what happened to it, we should respect its decisions about its own life: that animal would have a right to life. If it turned out that great apes or dolphins could make assessments about reasons for action, then they would have a right to life. But as far as we know, no non-human animals are capable of this: it is literally impossible for us to respect any animal's decision about its own life, because no animal can make such a decision.

Animal rights activists may be right that we are often influenced by our own interests when we think about whether it is wrong to kill animals for food or in the course of scientific experiments. But we can perfectly well consider cases in which human welfare is not involved.

Imagine a herd of baboons living in the wild that we know have an infectious and highly dangerous disease. We have no means of isolating this herd, and they will infect all the nearby animals unless we cull the sick. We should weigh up the harm of killing those animals against the benefit to the others of being saved from the disease. If the benefits outweigh the harms, we should go ahead and kill the sick animals. In fact, it might be wrong not to cull them, and put the other animals at risk. These animals have moral status – what happens to them matters morally – but they have no right to life.

By contrast, imagine that a group of humans have a similar infectious disease, and will make many of us ill if we do not intervene. We might be entitled to isolate these people to stop the disease spreading, but we are not entitled to kill them. We are not entitled to weigh up the benefits of saving the rest of us from the disease against the harm to them of being killed, because humans have a trump card: we must respect their decisions about their own life. Humans, unlike baboons, have a right to life.

Though animals do not have a right to life, it should be obvious that we are *not* always entitled to kill them. Killing an animal deprives it of all the good things it would have experienced in the rest of its life; we ought not to do so for a trivial reason. Even if animals have no right to life, it does *not* follow that we must be entitled to kill them for food, for example. Moreover, since death is worse for the more intellectually sophisticated animals, such as the great apes, it is worse to kill those creatures. But it is not wrong to kill an animal, terminally ill with a painful disease, that would not experience many goods in the rest of its life, because death does not deprive that animal of much that is good, even though the animal does not and could not give its consent to being killed.

Humans Who Cannot Make Decisions about Their Own Life

Most humans have the right to life, because for most of them death is bad and they do not consent to being killed. But some humans are not capable of understanding complex circumstances and assessing reasons: they are very young, or have severe mental disabilities. Like all animals, these humans cannot give or withhold their consent to anything. Just as there is no such thing as our respecting the judgement of animals about what happens in their lives, we cannot respect the judgements of these humans. In that sense, they cannot refuse to sacrifice their lives, and so they do not have a right to life in the same way that normal humans, who can make decisions about their own lives, do.

Obviously it is bad if these humans die, for they are deprived of the pleasures they would have enjoyed if they had lived for longer. We ought not to kill these humans as we ought not to kill animals, though our reasons for not killing humans will be stronger than our reasons not to kill animals whenever we would deprive the humans of more goods by a premature death. In many cases, we also have very powerful additional reasons not to kill humans.

Some humans cannot make judgements about their life in the present but will be able to do so in the future. Normal human babies cannot make these decisions but they will grow up to be adults who have the potential to understand complex situations and give or withhold their consent. Since they are sentient, human babies have moral status; what happens to them matters morally. It therefore matters morally whether they fulfil their potential to become fully responsible adults who deserve our respect. The parents of these babies have a duty to do as much as they can to help their children achieve their potential: to look after their children when they are sick and to help them to become independent and able to make their own decisions as they grow older. The rest of us do not have special obligations to bring up other people's children, but we do have a duty not to stop them achieving all that they can: we ought not to stand in their way. It would be very wrong for us to kill a normal healthy child, because we would cut short their life before they could realise their potential.

Some babies are born with brain damage, and may never be able to think about their own future or reflect on what matters to them. When we are uncertain whether a baby will develop normally, we should act on the assumption that he or she does have the potential, so that, at the very least, we do not prevent the baby from achieving what he or she can. It would be wrong to kill a brain-damaged human baby even if there were only a remote possibility that he or she might develop into a fully reflective adult.

There are normal adult humans, capable of reflection and judgement, who lose this capacity as they grow older and become ill. Suppose that Peter suffers from Alzheimer's disease. In the early stages of the disease, he was quite forgetful, but he could still enjoy his life: he liked talking to his children and grandchildren. At this stage, Peter was able to reflect on his life and evaluate it, and therefore we should have respected his own judgements about his life and, as far as we could, we ought not to have forced him to do things to which he did not consent. However, now he is suffering from the later stages of Alzheimer's, Peter can no longer make decisions about his own life at all. Similarly, suppose that Susan has been involved in a terrible car accident and has fallen into a coma from which she will probably never waken. Peter and Susan could once make reflective judgements about their lives but we know that they probably never will be able to do so again. How should we treat them?

Sometimes people make their wishes clear about what they would want to happen to them were they to become incapable of making their own decisions. We should respect those judgements, and where possible follow their wishes. If they have not made known their wishes, it still makes sense for us to try to decide what they would have consented to have happen to them if they had thought about falling into a coma. We should take account of their wish to be kept alive in such circumstances, or their preference to be allowed to die.

Peter and Susan will probably never again be capable of making decisions for themselves. Some human babies are born with such terrible brain damage that we can be certain that they never have been and never will be capable of reflecting on anything at all. Whenever there are humans who are not and will never be capable of reflection, we need to take into account what is in their interests – is their life worth living? – as well as what their parents and relatives want. If we consider that their life is worth living and their parents want them to be kept alive, we should respect their decision.

Some people think that all human life is sacred and should be preserved in all circumstances. But it is hard to see why human life as such should be more important than the lives of animals. Nevertheless, there are important differences between normal humans and other animals: normal humans have the capacity to make reflective judgements about their own lives that the rest of us should respect. In addition, though some humans, like all animals, may not be able to make this kind of judgement, it is usually worse to kill them than to kill animals. Human babies have or may have the potential to develop into independent, reflective adults who can make their own decisions; normal animals do not have this potential. Some humans used to have the capacity to make their own decisions but now this capacity is impaired or non-existent; we ought to respect their previous judgements about what they would choose in these circumstances. No animal has ever had the capacity to make these judgements. Finally, we need to take into account the decisions of the relatives of the unfortunate humans about whether they should be kept alive or allowed to die, whereas no animals have relatives that could make considered judgements about them.

It will usually be worse to kill a human than an animal for these reasons, even when the human has similar mental capacities to the animal. We have good non-prejudiced reasons to treat humans differently from animals, reasons that are based on the significant differences between most humans and other animals.

The argument of this chapter proves that it is a very complicated question when, if at all, it is morally acceptable to kill a human being or animal. It is a mistake to think that the matter is resolved when we decide whether or not a creature has the right to life. The right to life is a 'trump card' that means that we must not kill the right-holder even if many others would benefit greatly by his or her death. This trump card is based on the moral requirement that we respect people's judgements about their own life, particularly when we are considering doing them great harm, and so applies only to those who can make judgements about their own lives. Consequently, campaigners for animal welfare would be well advised not to concentrate too much on the case for animal rights. But there are many other considerations that we must take into account too, including the quantity of different kinds of goods that the creature would have enjoyed had it not died prematurely. In debates about the proper treatment of animals, it is vital that we pay attention to the forceful reasons against killing animals and in favour of promoting animal welfare, rather than focussing solely on the issue of rights.

CHAPTER TEN

ALL ANIMALS ARE
EQUAL ...?

Anna Sewell wrote only one book in her whole life, completing it just before her death in 1878. A devout Quaker, she hoped that her novel would contribute to the campaign against animal cruelty. Her wish was fulfilled: the impact of the book was huge. It sold more than 30 million copies, and is still loved by readers today.

The book was *Black Beauty*. Subtitled *The Autobiography of a Horse*, the novel is narrated from the animal's point of view, as he is sold from owner to owner, treated more and more badly, until he finally finds contentment at the end of his life.

Black Beauty is intended to be propaganda for the better treatment of animals, and it undoubtedly gains some of its power from echoes, conscious or unconscious, of another great crusade, the campaign against slavery; it is often compared to Harriet Beecher Stowe's influential anti-slavery novel *Uncle Tom's Cabin*. The structure of the book is similar to a 'slave narrative'. Black Beauty, who is identified by his colour and often referred to as 'Darkie', suffers under the yoke of a variety of different masters, good and bad, and is terribly injured at the whim of a drunk. His story is intertwined with that of Ginger, a more rebellious horse who stands up for herself, and as a consequence, fares much worse. Ginger is eventually worked and whipped until she longs for death as a release from her pain.

Animal rights protestors have long drawn analogies between their struggle and the fight for the abolition of slavery and for women's emancipation, and compared their opponents to the racists and sexists who resisted those movements. As we have finally come to recognise the essential equality of mankind, they argue, we ought to accept that all animals are equal too.

Sexism, Racism and Equal Rights

If you have moral status, then anything that harms you matters morally; if you do not have moral status, nothing that happens to you is morally important. Everything that has moral status has equal moral status: if a sentient animal and a human both suffer by the same amount, their distress is of equal moral significance. There is a sense, therefore, in which all (sentient) animals are morally equal.

Many people think that all humans have equal moral status but that they also have equal rights. Of course, in many past societies equal rights for all humans would have been considered ridiculous. Aristotle thought it obvious that morally good people were more worthy and were owed more than the wicked, and that natural slaves, people who were incapable of looking after themselves, had no rights at all. Many societies have found it natural that men, mistakenly believed to be the 'naturally superior' sex, should have more rights than women. There are very noticeable differences between individuals: some are prettier, cleverer, stronger, wiser or morally better than others. Surely it is surprising that even though we are not equal in all these important respects, we should be moral equals and have equal rights.

When we claim that people have equal rights, we usually do not mean that they are exactly equal in all these other ways. We do not have to deny that some people are prettier than others and some are cleverer than others. We can even accept that there are differences between groups of people: perhaps most men are naturally stronger than most women. All we need to claim is that in certain key areas, there is no morally significant difference between people of different sexes or races.

It is obvious that whether someone is male or female is a biologically significant feature of them: there are many respects in which men and women are different. And these differences affect how you should treat them; it is quite acceptable to treat men and women differently in some circumstances. What is wrong with sexism is that a sexist treats men and women differently when their sex does not matter. It is sexist to pay women less for doing the same job as a man when their abilities and skills at doing the job are identical; when men and women do equal work, there should be no difference in their pay. It is sexist to deny women the vote, when they are as capable as many of the men who are already permitted to vote of understanding the significance of political questions and using their vote sensibly. Even if it were true, as some sexists wrongly believe, that on average men are more able than women to understand politics, women are plainly intelligent enough to qualify for the vote. When women claim the right to vote or the right to equal pay for the same work, they need not claim that they are the same as men in all ways: they need only say that they are the same in respect of the quality needed for that right: the ability to work or to use a vote.

It would be absurd to claim that animals ought to have the right to vote and the right to equal pay for equal work. In the key respects, the ability to use a vote, the ability to do a particular paid job, animals are not the equals of humans. No one ever thought that they were, and defenders of animal rights never claimed anything so ridiculous. Some animal rights activists say that animals, like humans, have the right to life, because they are equal in this respect: death is bad for animals just as it is for humans. But in the last chapter, it was argued that there are differences between humans and animals that are crucial to the right to life. It is typically worse for a human to die prematurely than an animal, because the human will usually miss out on a wider range of more valuable goods than the animal. The human right to life is also based on the capacities of humans to give and withhold their consent to what happens to them in their lives: we ought to respect other people's judgements about their own life, and in particular we ought not to treat them badly against their will. If any animal had these capacities, it would have the right to life; but as far as we know, no animal does. Though it is bad to kill animals without good reason, they do not have the right to life because they are not the equals of humans in the ways relevant to the right to life. It is not biased or prejudiced to deny that humans and animals have equal rights.

Speciesism

Racists often deny that people of different races have equal rights but racism is sometimes defined more broadly, as a kind of bias or prejudice: it is racist to treat some person differently from another merely because of his or her race. Recently there has been much debate about 'positive discrimination' on behalf of a previously oppressed group, for example, using a quota system to ensure that a certain percentage of people who join a university or police force are of a particular race. If positive discrimination is justified at all, it is because it partially rectifies injustices that have been carried out in the past to people of a certain race or because it counteracts on-going discrimination. When positive discrimination is justified, race is not morally irrelevant, because injustices have been, and maybe still are, targeted at a particular racial group.

There are times when it may be right to treat people differently on the basis of their race or sex. Racism and sexism are wrong not because people should *never* be treated differently on the basis of their race or sex, but because they should not be treated differently when their race or sex is *irrelevant*.

Speciesism is, according to Peter Singer, 'a prejudice or attitude of bias towards the interests of one's own species and against those of members of other species'. If you cared about whether humans were killed, but not whether animals were killed, simply because they were not of your species, you would be guilty of speciesism.

The term 'speciesism' is supposed to emphasise the links between speciesism, racism and sexism; since most people think that sexism and racism are wrong, they are likely to think speciesism is wrong too. But is the analogy valid?

If species were a morally significant category, it could be appropriate for us to treat other creatures worse than we treat humans: speciesism would not be wrong. Different species of animals have a variety of needs and wants and it is entirely appropriate to treat animals that have diverse basic needs and preferences differently. No sensible person would treat a snake, a flea, a hippopotamus and a canary in exactly the same way: they need different kinds and quantities of food, and totally different living conditions. The species of an animal is often related to what the animal wants and needs: a difference of species can be correlated with features of an animal that are morally relevant. But can a difference of species carry moral significance by itself?

First we need to know what it means for two animals to be of the same species. Biologists disagree about exactly how to answer this question, but most say that it depends on whether the animals are able to mate together and produce fertile offspring: two horses are of the same species because they can mate successfully; you and I are of the same species because we can mate together. If species were a morally relevant feature of animals, it would have to matter morally whether or not two animals could successfully mate. But why on earth would *that* be morally relevant?

Imagine that another species evolved at the same time as us, the species human*. Humans* have remarkably similar mental capacities to us, they look exactly like us, and they even have similar cultures and societies: humans and humans* can talk together, live together and work together. But we cannot reproduce together. It would be surprising if we ought to treat humans* differently from humans just because we cannot have children with them. We might find that we felt a stronger bond with humans than with humans* (though perhaps not, if humans* looked just like us and shared our culture). But however we felt about humans*, surely we *ought* to treat them just as we would treat humans. A difference in species by itself cannot matter morally.

Friends, Family and Species

Must we think only about an individual animal's needs and wants when we decide how to treat it? When we consider how to treat other humans, it is obvious that we take many other things into account. In particular, we spend a lot more time on our friends and family than we do on strangers. We think it important to pay them more attention than strangers, for if we did not, we could not have meaningful relationships with them at all.

We don't accuse people who have friends of 'friendism', of a prejudice of treating people who happen to be their own friends disproportionately better than strangers. We think that it is natural and good to have friendships, and it is right to look out for your friends. Of course, this does not mean that you should entirely neglect everyone else, treat strangers really badly or favour your friends and family in every circumstance, but sometimes it is perfectly acceptable to give them extra consideration.

We feel a natural bond towards members of our own species, other humans, particularly when they are under threat. We feel that they are our kin, if a more distant kin than our friends and family. Imagine that you are passing a burning house. You manage to go in to check whether anyone is still inside, and see a baby and a parrot in a cage. Suppose that you can only carry one of them out. Which do you save?

Of course, you save the baby. It would be odd if you even had to think about your answer. When a human and a non-human are under threat, you choose to save the human: it is natural to feel most concern for the member of your own species. This bias is not unique to humans: a special concern for their own species seems to be natural for many animals.

If It's Natural Is It Right?

A feeling or a way of behaving is natural for us if it is common to many humans who are brought up in very different circumstances and in very different cultures. It may be natural for us to bond with members of our own species more than with members of any other species, just as chimps bond with other chimps, dogs with dogs and so on.

This may lead us to care more for other humans than for non-human animals and to treat animals differently on the basis of their species: we naturally treat most other humans better than most non-human animals, just as we favour our friends and family over strangers.

But unlike other species, we humans are capable of altering our natural behaviour on the basis of what we think is right. Just because some behaviour is natural to us, it is not automatically either right or wrong. It may be natural for us to care a lot about our children, which is good, because we look after them more carefully. It may be natural for us to be too selfish, which is bad, because we are simply unmoved by other people's suffering even when it would cost us very little to help them. Our natural behaviour can be good, but often it is not.

Even if we do care for humans much more than for other animals, we can ask ourselves whether we are right to do so, just as we can ask ourselves whether we are right to benefit our friends and family over strangers. If we decide that we favour our friends too much, we can take steps to change the way we act towards them, showing more consideration for the basic needs of strangers, and less for the whims of our friends. Similarly, if we decide that it is wrong to treat humans better than animals, or at least that it is wrong to treat them so much better than we treat animals, we can at least try to pay greater attention to the needs of animals, and less to the minor concerns of humans.

Suppose that it is natural for us to bond more closely with other humans than with animals and to treat humans better;

it is natural for us to be speciesist. Speciesism can be compared to racism and sexism, and it can be compared to a special concern for family and friends. But most of us think that whereas caring for one's friends and family is good, a particular concern for members of one's race or sex is not. We would judge speciesism to be good if it were like caring for friends and family, but bad if it were more similar to racism and sexism.

A bias towards one's friends is different from a bias towards one's race: they result in very different kinds of relationships. A special concern for our friends and family enables us to be very close to a few people. We know them very well, and they know us. We enjoy being in each other's company. We go on holiday with them, play sport together or share hobbies, join the same clubs. We could not have close friendships if we treated our friends no differently from strangers. So although we should not entirely neglect strangers for the sake of our friends, we *are* justified in treating our friends differently from strangers at least sometimes, because friendships are a hugely significant component of a good life.

Having a bias towards one's race or sex does not contribute to a special relationship with those people. Racists and sexists tend to have contempt for those not of their race or sex and usually treat them particularly badly, rather than, as in a friendship, treating some people particularly well and developing valuable bonds with them. The bias that racists and sexists have for their own race and sex does not contribute to their having a good life.

A special concern for one's species is most similar to racism and sexism. Speciesists tend to treat non-human animals particularly badly, rather than treating humans particularly well. A speciesist does not have a special relationship with his fellow humans: how could he when he has not even met most of them? Speciesism does not contribute to having a good life, in the way that having friendships does.

Even if it is natural for us to have a bias towards our own species, it is open to us to reconsider that concern and see whether it is justified. Defenders of animal rights are correct to say that a prejudice towards your own species is wrong, just as racism and sexism are wrong. They go on to conclude that animals and humans have equal rights, just as humans of all races and sexes have equal rights. But this is a mistake. Humans of all races and all sexes have equal rights because they are equal in the ways relevant to having those rights: they can use their vote, they can do the same jobs, they can give or withhold their consent to what happens to them. Animals are not equal to humans in these ways. It is wrong to treat non-human animals worse than humans merely because of their species. But because there are other differences between humans and other animals that are morally relevant, it is not true that all animals have equal rights.

Conclusion

The seventh and final commandment of *Animal Farm* – all animals are equal – was also the most important. But as we have seen, this claim oversimplifies a much more complex reality.

The ground of moral status is the capacity to feel pain and pleasure. Any animals that can feel pain have moral status: it matters morally when they suffer. Plants and non-sentient animals, by contrast, do not have moral status.

The death of a human is usually worse than the death of an animal, because we are typically deprived of more goods by a premature death. The more intellectually sophisticated the animal, the more it misses out on by an early death, and so the worse it is to kill that animal. It is therefore worse to kill a highly developed great ape than it is to kill a mollusc.

The right to life is like a 'trump' card that (usually) entitles its bearer to refuse to be killed in order to benefit others. Humans have a right to life because death is bad for us and we can withhold our consent to being killed. As far as we know, animals cannot give or withhold their consent to anything. So no animal has a right to life.

In one respect, we can endorse *Animal Farm*'s seventh commandment: humans and other animals are of equal moral status; an equal harm to each matters equally. But in other respects we cannot agree with it: typically it is worse to kill some animals than others and with regard to the right to life, humans and animals are not moral equals.

How should we treat animals that have moral status but no right to life? In the next part of the book we assess our most controversial uses of animals: farming for food, fox-hunting, and scientific experimentation. Are any of them acceptable; or should they all be banned?

PART THREE

HOW SHOULD WE

TREAT ANIMALS?

CHAPTER ELEVEN

FACTORY FOOD

'We are born, we are given just so much food as will keep the breath in our bodies … the very instant that our usefulness has come to an end we are slaughtered with hideous cruelty … The life of an animal is misery and slavery: that is the plain truth.'

Old Major, the prophesying pig of *Animal Farm*, bemoans the lot of a farm animal, before recounting his vision of a better life in a farm run by the animals themselves. But he was in fact lucky, even though he did not know it. He could not possibly have guessed what was in store for future generations of livestock, as traditional free-range farms turned into industrial factories for manufacturing food.

Many people buy meat from the supermarket every week knowing little or nothing about the conditions in which the animals they eat were kept when alive. Most supermarket meat now comes from factory farms. Chickens are farmed as 'broilers' for meat, and as 'battery hens' for eggs. Over 600 million broilers are killed each year in the UK, and there are over 33 million battery hens. Broilers are kept in huge windowless sheds in enormous flocks of 50,000–100,000 birds. Their food, water, temperature and ventilation are controlled automatically; the food contains growth-promoting antibiotics. The shed floor is covered in a layer of litter that is not changed throughout the lifetime of the bird. The birds are not caged, but have little space (about the size of one A4 piece of paper per bird); as they grow very fast, their shed becomes increasingly cramped. Often, their skeleton is unable to support their own weight, and up to 80 per cent of broilers suffer from broken bones; the birds that are the worst crippled die of hunger or thirst, unable to reach their food and water. Diseases spread easily in the crowded sheds; salmonella is particularly prevalent; about 6 per cent of birds die in the sheds. Broilers reach full size in just six or seven weeks and are slaughtered straightaway; twenty years ago it took them twice as long to reach that size. The natural life span of a chicken is six to seven years. Birds are often injured while they are captured in their sheds; they can get much too cold or hot during the transport to the slaughterhouse depending on the weather. They are usually stunned before they are killed, but the stunning is often inadequate and the birds can still be conscious when their necks are cut.

Battery hens live in similar sheds containing up to 30,000 birds in rows and rows of cages. These cages allow about two-thirds of the size of an A4 sheet of paper to each bird. Feeding and watering are automated; the food can contain the remains of unwanted male chicks as well as growth-promoting antibiotics. Hens kept in battery cages are unable to carry out their normal behaviour: wing-flapping, dust-bathing, scratching, pecking, and so on. The resulting frustration leads to aggressive behaviour: the hens often peck each other. To prevent this, the beaks of the birds are sometimes partially removed, but de-beaking is often carried out without anaesthetic and causes the birds distress. Diseases like salmonella are widespread in the overcrowded sheds. Because the hens cannot exercise, their bones are brittle and often break; because they cannot scratch their claws, these grow too long and can become entangled in the floor of the cage preventing the bird from getting to its food and water. As with the broilers, mortality is about 6 per cent in the battery sheds. These specially bred hens can produce 300 eggs a year; an astonishing increase from their wild ancestors that produced twelve to twenty. After twelve months their ability to lay eggs declines and they are slaughtered and used in processed food.

There are around 3 million dairy cows in the UK. Most graze on pasture during the spring and summer and are housed indoors in cowsheds for about seven months during the winter, though the practice of keeping them indoors for all of the year is increasing. Dairy cattle are kept almost constantly pregnant. Calves are usually taken away from their mother within 24 hours, and the cow is then milked two or three times a day for about ten months. Selective breeding and concentrated feeds have meant that dairy cows can produce ten times more milk than their calves would suckle. This overmilking results in up to a third of all dairy cattle each year suffering from mastitis, an infection of the udder that is potentially fatal, and from a variety of other diseases exacerbated by poor hygiene and overproduction,

Battery-farmed chickens

including BSE. Male calves, which cannot provide milk and are unsuitable to be raised as beef (dairy cattle are bred for high milk yields, not to produce high-quality beef), are 'by-products' of the dairy industry. The typical fate of these calves is to be raised as veal, by a process that has become notorious. Veal is prized for its soft white meat; to make the flesh of the calves soft they are fed only liquids and given no solid food in the whole of their short lives. To keep their flesh pale-coloured, they are housed in the dark and are deliberately made anaemic, fed only foods low in iron. They are kept in special wooden slatted crates too small for them to turn around in so that they cannot expend any energy moving. Five per cent of veal calves die in their first three weeks of life. Three weeks later, more than half of the surviving calves have a respiratory disease. In 1990 the use of veal crates was banned in the UK, where veal is in any case not popular; but dairy farmers in the UK transport their unwanted calves to continental Europe where veal is still highly valued and veal crates are still used.

Pigs are highly intelligent and social animals that traditionally lived in woodland, foraging for nuts and seeds. The pig industry in the UK is large, with about 9 million pigs reared each year in very intensive conditions. About half of the breeding sows are kept indoors, until recently either in barred stalls so narrow that the sow was unable to turn around, or tethered by a heavy chain attached to a strap around her neck or body. Lameness, leg, back and hip problems and sores are all common. Intensified rearing has led to increased disease problems, particularly among piglets; viral pneumonia and meningitis are common. On average, each sow produces 22 piglets per year and spends two-thirds of her life pregnant. After three or four years a sow is slaughtered for sausages, pork pies and other processed products. The piglets are usually slaughtered after four to seven months. The pigs are stunned before their throats are slit, but the stunning is not always effective. The natural lifespan of a pig is ten to fifteen years.

Is Factory Farming Morally Acceptable?

The Benefits of Factory Farming: Cheaper Meat
Factory farm workers do not keep animals in small pens and feed them growth-promoting chemicals because they enjoy

hurting animals; they do so because they are the optimal conditions to produce the fattest chickens, pigs and calves as quickly and cheaply as possible. It costs a lot to run a free-range farm where animals are kept in smaller numbers and allowed to roam free or are kept in large pens: factory farms produce meat much more efficiently. Consumers respond by buying these products, rather than more expensive meat from free-range animals: factory farms give the customers what they want.

In the past, meat was an expensive luxury; only the rich could afford to eat it regularly. Factory farms provide cheap meat so that all the people who could not have bought meat every day now can do so.

Why does it matter whether eating meat is the preserve of the rich? There are two main reasons why it might be important that the less well off can eat meat: because it is good for them; and because they want to do so.

Is it really good for people to eat meat? Meat is a good source of protein and of minerals such as iron; it is easier for some people to eat well if they eat some meat as well as vegetables. But it is not essential for most people to eat meat to keep healthy. In fact, there is now plenty of evidence that most vegetarians can be as healthy if not more so than meat-eaters: vegetarians tend to have lower cholesterol, and are less likely to suffer from diabetes, heart attacks and certain kinds of cancer.

Factory farming gives people what they want: those who could not buy meat produced in other ways can afford the cheaper meat; those who could have bought more expensively produced meat can purchase cheaper factory-farmed meat and have money left over for whatever else they desire. If factory farming were banned, both groups of people would be somewhat more miserable, because they could not eat meat as often or as cheaply as before. But this would not be too great a cost for them to bear. In addition, it would be possible for a government to subsidise free-range farms so that the meat produced by such farms was not as expensive as it is now. Issues of the cost of meat would no longer be so important. Factory-farmed food would have no significant benefits over free-range farmed meat.

The Costs of Factory Farms: Animal Suffering
It is difficult to see pictures of a factory farm, the huge industrial shed, the rows of tiny wire cages crammed with birds, the dead and dying creatures, without thinking that this is an extremely peculiar life for an animal. Chickens should be pecking about in the dust outside a farmhouse in the countryside, not trapped in an industrial space too small to spread their wings. Many people's strongest objection to modern farming is that factory farms seem so unnatural.

What does it mean to say that a type of farming is unnatural? We often contrast the natural and the artificial: natural things would be the same as they are now if there were no humans or if humans had not interfered with them; artificial things would not exist or would be different if there were no humans or if humans had not intervened. The moon, the Victoria Falls, the Grand Canyon are natural; televisions, the Taj Mahal, and a cheeseburger with fries are artificial.

Farm animals like cows, sheep, pigs and chickens have been bred by farmers for thousands of years. They are alive today in part because of the choices made by farmers in the past about which animals should breed together. These farmers selected animals that had useful characteristics: that tasted best, that fattened quickly and that were easy to look after. Farm animals are natural in a sense of course: they are living organisms that are part of the natural world. But the kind of creatures that they are has been influenced for many years by human desires and decisions.

Factory-farmed animals are often bred for a life of factory farming; they are not animals brought up on a traditional farm that have been kidnapped and placed in conditions unlike any they previously knew. Most factory-farmed animals never know anything other than what it is like inside their own shed, many never see the sun or a field in the countryside. Of course, it was not inevitable that factory-farmed animals would live in a factory farm. If the farm owners had made a different decision, the animal might have been killed immediately, or might have lived its life on a traditional farm. But in what sense is it unnatural to keep an animal in the conditions of a factory farm? You might say that if humans had not intervened, no animals would have been living in tiny cages without sunlight. But if farmers had not made their selections, there would be no chickens, pigs or cows as we know them now either. If humans had not interfered with other animals at all, there would be no farms of any kind. Both traditional free-range farms and factory farms are artificial in the sense that they would not have existed if there were no humans: in this respect factory farms are no more unnatural than traditional free-range farms.

Another sense of 'natural' distinguishes what humans do in any society from what is 'cultural', dependent on a particular cultural setting. It may be natural for humans to eat food, but what food they eat depends on their culture. Traditional forms of farming are more natural in the sense that they have existed in a wider range of cultures than have factory farms. But even if factory farms are less natural than traditional farms, is this an objection to them? Not everything that is unnatural is bad: it may be that in very few societies, men treat women with respect, but it is obviously not bad when they do. Factory farming is not morally worse just because it is found in only a few cultures.

Objecting to factory farms on the grounds that they are unnatural is no use. In the first place, all forms of farming are in a sense unnatural, and secondly, not everything that is unnatural is therefore bad.

But factory farms do keep animals in conditions that cause them distress and suffering: this is the real reason why factory farms are morally worse than traditional free-range farms.

We can be confident, for the reasons given in Chapter 3, that the kinds of animals that are factory farmed – chickens, pigs and cows – can feel pain. But though we can be sure that these animals can suffer, we should not be so confident that we know when they are in distress. It is easy to think that factory-farmed animals suffer in the same way that humans would if they were kept in cramped conditions in a steel barn and constantly fed chemicals. But this may be a mistake: animals bred to live on a factory farm may not suffer from being caged as humans would, for they cannot understand what it means to lose their freedom and they have been bred to be docile and content: they are certainly not as frightened as wild animals would be in the same circumstances. Nevertheless, factory farms clearly do make animals suffer: they are kept in very unhygienic surroundings, without clean air to breathe and in such cramped conditions that diseases easily spread. They are often sick and many of them die. Hens that are unable to carry out their natural behaviour of pecking, dust-bathing and so on are often visibly distressed.

Even though factory-farmed animals are bred for life on the farm, factory farming causes much more suffering than does free-range farming, for no significant extra benefits, and so it is morally worse. If we have the choice between buying free-range meat and buying factory-farmed meat, we certainly should not purchase the products from factory farms.

A factory farmer might object to these claims as follows: suppose that farming is morally acceptable, that it is not wrong to raise animals with the intention of killing and eating them. If farming is permitted, surely regulations about how you keep the animal before you kill it are mere cosmetic window-dressing. Isn't it hypocritical to worry about the size of a chicken's cage when you know you are going to slaughter it in a few weeks anyway? So if farming animals for food is permitted at all, factory farming should be allowed too.

It is a terrible mistake to think that it does not matter what happens to an animal before it is killed. In factory farms, animals are kept in conditions that cause them considerable suffering. It is bad that creatures of moral status suffer, whatever happens to them in the future. So it is incorrect to say that if animals are killed, their life beforehand is of no consequence and their pain during that life does not matter. It is morally worse for the animals to suffer than for them to have a happy life free from pain even if afterwards they are killed.

Factory farming is morally worse than traditional free-range farming, because factory-farmed animals suffer more than animals on free-range farms. Though it is always difficult to work out how much animals suffer, and to weigh up their suffering against human pleasures, it seems overwhelmingly likely that factory farming imposes far more suffering on animals than it benefits us. Animals are treated so badly in factory farming that it should not be allowed to continue in its present form. There should be much stricter regulations in farming to raise the standards of animal welfare, even if the cost of meat must rise as a consequence, and in the meantime, none of us should support factory farms by buying meat produced under factory farm conditions.

Is Eating Meat Ever Morally Acceptable?

The Benefits of Eating Meat: Nature, Culture, Health and Pleasure

If it were necessary for us to eat meat to have a healthy diet, we would surely be entitled to do so, to ensure that we might stay alive and flourish. In some parts of the world, where plants do not thrive, it is difficult to survive on a vegetarian diet. If we are in the unusual circumstances of needing to eat meat to survive, we may eat meat; but of course most of us could survive and would even be healthier on a vegetarian diet; we do not *need* to eat meat at all.

Some might argue that it *must* be acceptable for us to eat meat because it is *natural* for us to do so. Humans seem to have evolved as omnivores, eating a diet of meat and plants. But we have seen many times already that what is natural for us to do may not be right: like racism and sexism, meat-eating may be natural but wrong.

Eating meat is not just natural for us, however, it is also culturally important: many cultures and religions put a lot of emphasis on preparing and eating special kinds of food. Roast beef, fish and chips, and egg and bacon breakfasts are traditional British foods. Jewish families always eat lamb at Passover. These practices are important to our sense of identity as members of a particular culture or religion. Since many people think that we ought to support different cultural and religious traditions, oughtn't we to encourage meat-eating too?

If a cultural or religious practice involves doing something harmful and wrong, it is not acceptable to carry on with it however long and venerable its tradition. Instead, the harmful part of the practice should be outlawed, the remaining aspects of it should be retained. For example, a crucial element of the ancient Roman religion was the ritual sacrifice of bulls, goats and other animals, through which the Romans believed they could communicate with the gods. Animal sacrifices were often symbolically replaced with cakes shaped as animals that were much cheaper to provide than live animals. The Romans were prepared to alter their ritual so that it did not include the actual killing of animals (though for reasons of cost rather than animal welfare), and the modified ritual could play the same important role for them. Just because eating meat is part of our culture does not mean that we must continue to be carnivorous.

Many people have jobs in the meat industry, in farms, vets, slaughterhouses, butchers and supermarkets, that would be lost if everyone became a vegetarian or if free-range as well as factory farming were banned. They would lose their means of support, which would be bad for them, their families and their communities too. Some of them might find jobs in similar fields, but many probably could not. The cost to these people would be considerable if we all became vegetarian. But on the other hand, if eating meat and raising animals for food are morally wrong, people ought not to make money out of them. The fact that thousands of jobs depend on the meat industry does not mean that we must all support it by eating meat.

The main benefit to us of eating meat is obviously that many of us enjoy it. That is why eating meat is a part of so many cultures and religious traditions, and why the vast majority of us are not vegetarians, despite the increase in its popularity in recent years. Our enjoyment of eating meat need not be cruel, for we are *not* taking pleasure in killing animals or causing them suffering (indeed many of us go out of our way to *avoid* being reminded that animals must die for our food). Eating meat is a genuine benefit to us. On the other hand, it is a benefit that we could live without. Are we morally entitled to buy and eat meat and to farm animals for food?

The Cost of Eating Meat: Lack of Respect

If you came across an animal that had died of natural causes, and you were not responsible for its death, would there be anything wrong with eating its meat? Some might argue that even when you had neither killed the animal nor caused it to suffer, it would nevertheless be wrong to eat the animal. After all it would be unthinkable for most of us to eat a dead human in the same circumstances. Obviously eating the dead animal would not harm it, for it can no longer suffer. But, it might be argued, it would still be wrong to eat it, for you would be *expressing a lack of respect* towards the animal. Eating an animal might express the view that you are entitled to use the animal for your own enjoyment; and just as we ought not to use animals in any way we choose, we also ought not to act in ways that symbolically express that we may do so.

172

It is true that we often think that the way we treat the body of a person after they are dead can express respect to them: that is why people in many different cultures place so much importance on carrying out ceremonies for their dead relatives and friends and most would be revolted by the idea of eating a human body. But in different cultures, the ceremonial treatment of the dead is quite different. In some cultures the dead are buried, in some their bodies are burnt, in some their bodies are left to be eaten by vultures. There is no single way of treating the bodies of the dead that expresses respect towards them; one might burn a person's body respectfully or without showing any respect. There is nothing in particular about eating an animal that expresses either respect or a lack of respect towards it: it is possible to carry out the same activity with either attitude. It need not be wrong to eat meat, at least when you are not responsible for the death of the animal.

So eating meat is not always wrong: it is morally acceptable in certain circumstances. But this does not show that eating meat from farmed animals is morally acceptable; for in buying farmed meat, even free-range farmed meat, you are supporting an industry that imposes death on millions of animals. Is it ever acceptable to eat meat from farms?

The Costs of Eating Meat: the Harms to Farm Animals
If we all gave up eating animals, in the future there would be far fewer chickens, cows, pigs and sheep alive, because we would not breed large numbers of them as our food. Some good does come from eating meat for the farm

animals themselves: if no one ate meat, most of these animals would never have lived at all. If the animals have a life worth living, they benefit from our support of farms and our eating meat.

This argument could not be used to defend factory farming, as it is highly unlikely that factory-farmed animals do have a life worth living. But the argument has force in support of free-range farming, provided that free-range farmed animals do have a worthwhile life. Of course, all farm animals typically have a much shorter life than they would if they were not farmed, for they are slaughtered as soon as they reach maximum weight. They may also suffer more than they would have done if they had not been farmed: even free-range animals are often kept in confined conditions and may be more prone to diseases; they certainly can suffer when they are transported to slaughter and sometimes too when they are killed (especially if they are not properly stunned beforehand). But it is reasonable to think that their lives are nonetheless worth living, that it is good for them that they exist, and that far fewer of them would have lived at all if we did not have farms and we did not eat meat.

Nevertheless, we would obviously object strongly to a system of human farms, where humans were bred, brought up and slaughtered for food, and surely we could make a parallel argument in favour of farm humans: 'these humans would die at some point in time; all we are doing is intervening so that they die sooner rather than later. Farm humans have a life worth living, and many of them would

not have lived at all if we did not have this farming system.'
It would be monstrous to farm humans for food; how can it
be acceptable to farm animals?

As we saw in Chapters 9 and 10, it is typically much worse
to kill a human than it is to kill an animal. Humans enjoy a
much wider range of goods, and more valuable goods, than
do animals. When humans die prematurely, we miss out
on a greater variety of experiences than do animals: we
typically have many plans and projects that are frustrated,
we are deprived of the opportunity to develop mature,
intimate, valuable relationships, and so on. Animals that die
early, by contrast, miss out on a few simple pleasures, but
that is all. In addition, humans typically do not give their
consent to be killed. Since killing a human is typically much
worse than killing an animal, it is deeply misleading to
compare human and animal farming. It would be wrong to
farm humans, because it would be wrong to cut short a
human life even if you immediately brought into existence a
replacement human who also had a worthwhile life: it
would violate the first human's right to life. But it is not
necessarily wrong to kill animals, especially when at the
same time you breed replacement animals that also have
lives worth living; this cannot violate any animal's right to
life, for no animals have such a right. Whether it is morally
acceptable to support free-range animal farming depends
on whether humans and animals overall benefit by the practice. If the benefits to humans and to farm animals outweigh
the harms imposed by any large-scale farming, then free-
range farming is acceptable; otherwise it is not.

Is It Wrong to Kill Animals for Food?

Death is bad for an animal, because it deprives that animal of all of the goods it would have had if it had not died prematurely. It is acceptable to kill an animal only if the benefits to humans and other animals outweigh this harm to the animal itself. To decide whether it is morally acceptable to kill animals for food, we have to weigh up these harms and benefits. On the negative side is the harm we do to the farmed animal, which is typically deprived of several years of life it might have enjoyed, and which may also suffer from disease or maltreatment even in a free-range farm. On the positive side is our enjoyment in eating meat; and also the benefit to the chickens, cows, sheep and pigs that live a worthwhile life for at least a short while, which would not have been born at all if we did not farm animals for food. It is very hard to measure and to compare these harms and benefits: whether we are entitled to eat meat may turn out to depend on the kind of animal, and the exact details of the way it is farmed and slaughtered.

For example, it is questionable whether shellfish are sentient at all, whether they have any experiences, pleasant or unpleasant. If they are not sentient, there is nothing at all wrong with killing them for food.

The brains of fish do not seem to be sufficiently developed for fish to have a complex mental life. It seems likely that fish may be sentient but have at best a primitive mind. Killing a fish deprives it only of simple experiences; this harm to the fish may be outweighed by the enjoyment to humans of eating it. In addition, we can expect that fish that live wild before they are caught enjoy their natural life; we impose no suffering on them at all until they are netted. Increasingly, however, as the stocks of fish in the oceans are depleted, we are turning to farming popular fish such as salmon. The welfare problems of farmed fish are similar to those of factory-farmed chickens, cows and pigs: the fish are kept at very high density and diseases are rife. It is possible too for the fish to be contaminated by polluted water, and to pose a risk to human health when we eat them. For the sake of our own health and for animal welfare reasons, we ought to eat wild rather than farmed fish.

Unfortunately, catching some wild fish such as tuna carries with it a risk of killing other marine creatures including dolphins that have an impressively complex mental life. Dolphins are deprived of more by death than are fish, and we should use only those methods of tuna fishing that do not risk killing them.

Is it wrong to kill farm animals – chickens, pigs, cows and sheep – for food? These animals seem to have a more complex mental life than fish, but less than dolphins. Are the goods that they are deprived of in death greater than the benefits we gain from eating them and the benefits they gain from having lived a brief, but worthwhile life (assuming that they enjoy living on a free-range farm)? This question is very difficult to answer, and reasonable people may disagree about what is the right response. I think that, in at least some circumstances, it is acceptable to kill free-range farm animals for food. Many humans certainly enjoy eating meat and, since this need not be a cruel pleasure, it should be included in the sum of the harms and benefits of free-range farming. Though the animals will almost inevitably suffer during transportation and slaughter, they can have lives worth living. These lives are cut short when they are slaughtered, but the farmer breeds new animals to replace them that have lives worth living too; overall, free-range farmed animals can benefit from the practice of farming, for without it they most likely would not have lived at all. It seems to me that the benefits of free-range farming can outweigh the costs, and so it can be morally acceptable to eat free-range meat.

It is possible, however, that this evaluation of these costs and benefits is mistaken, that *any* commercial farming imposes suffering on animals so great that it outweighs the benefits to them of life itself and the benefits to us of eating meat, in which case even free-range farming would be wrong, and it would always be morally wrong to farm animals for food.

Some people who do not eat the flesh of animals also do not drink milk or eat other dairy products. In principle, we can eat dairy products without harming animals; in these circumstances, there is nothing wrong with our use of them. In practice, however, most current dairy farming is a kind of factory farming, in which cows are bred to produce enormous quantities of milk and their calves are slaughtered.

The same objections to eating meat produced by factory farming also apply to drinking factory-farmed milk. It can be acceptable to drink milk and eat dairy products, but only when they are not produced by methods of farming that inflict such suffering on so many animals.

CHAPTER TWELVE

FOXHUNTING

'Foxhunting is the sport of kings, the image of war without its guilt and only five-and-twenty per cent of its danger.' So wrote Robert Smith Surtees in his 1843 novel *Handley Cross, or Mr Jorrocks' Hunt.* Huntsman and comic writer, precursor of Dickens, Surtees wrote several novels recounting the sporting adventures of Jorrocks, the cockney grocer, as well as others with titles like *Mr Facey Romford's Hounds* and *Mr Sponge's Sporting Tour.*

The idea that foxhunting is somehow comparable to warfare is quite common among huntsmen, who claim to admire and respect the cunning of the fox, as one might appreciate the manoeuvres of a rival general. But there cannot have been many wars as one-sided as a typical foxhunt, which pits some 30 riders and their hounds against a single quarry with no weapons of its own and no chance to counterattack, that can hope at best to outrun or outwit its enemy and escape with its life. Estimating the dangers of a hunt as a quarter of those of a war looks somewhat excessive with regard to the riders and their dogs, but remarkably optimistic from the point of view of the fox.

A typical foxhunt lasts all day, beginning in the morning

as the hounds set off, searching for the scent of a fox to follow. The fox is sometimes 'chopped': found and killed instantly without a chase. Otherwise, the hounds pursue the fox with the riders following at a distance, unable to keep up. The chase can last from a few minutes to over an hour, but the average is fifteen to twenty minutes. When the dogs catch the fox, they bring it down and kill it very quickly, tearing at the carcass until the riders catch up and call them off.

Before the hunt begins, volunteers block up the foxholes to prevent the fox from escaping the chase. If the fox finds an uncovered hole and goes to ground, a terrier is sent down after it to 'flush' it out, and it is either chased again or shot immediately.

In November 2004, against considerable opposition, the British parliament banned hunting with hounds. At the time there were 175 registered foxhunting packs in England and Wales. Foxhunts took place between August and April and 20,000–25,000 foxes were killed each year; on average, each hunt killed one fox during each day of hunting. It is likely that more foxes than this were killed because unregistered hunts took place as well.

Most of the arguments made here about hunting rely on information from the *Burns Report*, commissioned by the British government to investigate the pros and cons of hunting. There are significant problems in trying to decide whether the UK parliament was right to ban foxhunting because many of the facts of the case are in dispute. It is controversial whether there are good reasons to cull foxes,

Foxhunting: the image of war without the guilt?

how much the fox suffers during the hunt and how much it would suffer if it were killed by an alternative method. Since these key facts about foxhunting are not yet known, at best we can draw only provisional conclusions about the morality of hunting.

The Culture of Hunting

Surtees was quite right that kings are keen on foxhunting: Edward I had a pack of foxhounds in the 13th century; and hunting has been a popular pastime for the nobility for hundreds of years. The defenders of hunting identify strongly with this countryside tradition.

Hunting is clearly a minority culture, but in other contexts, many people think that minority cultures should be encouraged and supported rather than outlawed, because living in a country with diverse cultures is simply more interesting than living in a wholly homogeneous community. Though few people speak Welsh compared with other languages, there have been campaigns to prevent Welsh-speaking from dying out, for the Welsh culture has a long and rich history that might be forgotten if the language was neglected and allowed to wither. Many people identify themselves specifically as Welsh, and it is immensely valuable for them to be able to connect with their forebears by speaking the same tongue. This obviously does not mean that everyone ought to take up speaking Welsh, but we should at least not put obstacles in the way of those who want to speak the language.

Foxhunting has a long history, its own language, customs, and very distinctive costumes. It is not surprising that followers of the hunt identify with its traditions, feeling that they are participating in a practice special to the British countryside and that hunt protestors are townspeople who are ignorant of country life. In Spain, supporters of bull-fighting have made a similar defence of their sport, arguing that it is part of the Spanish identity, and that it deserves to be protected as an important cultural practice with a rich history.

But, as we saw in discussing the cultural importance of food, a culture is valuable, no matter what its history, no matter how many people participate in it and how much they identify with it, *only* if it is morally acceptable. It may be good to live in a society that includes a variety of customs, but not when the diversity includes morally deplorable cultures. The custom of lynch mobs in the racist southern states of America may have had a long history lying behind it, and no doubt some Americans identified strongly with it, but we should all be extremely glad that that culture has died out.

Many cultural practices have some aspects that are morally questionable and some that are not. The morally questionable part of foxhunting is the chasing and killing of a fox. Of course hunt supporters claim that the kill is justified and that hunting is morally acceptable. But even if they are not correct about this, there are many elements of the hunt that are not morally wrong: there is nothing wrong with wearing special clothes, meeting with other people who are similarly dressed, riding round the countryside on horses (provided you have permission from the owners of the land) or following a trail with dogs. Drag hunting is an alternative to foxhunting that involves using horses and hounds to follow a scent-trail that has been laid down earlier in the day by human volunteers. The only elements of foxhunting that drag hunting does not incorporate are the morally questionable ones: the chasing and killing of a fox.

If hunters prefer foxhunting to drag hunting as a form of entertainment, as they plainly do, it must be because they particularly enjoy the chasing and killing of a fox. Even though foxhunting clearly gives pleasure to its participants, we ought not to weigh their gratification against the cost to the fox, because their pleasure is cruel: it is *essentially* connected to harming the fox. Since it is wrong to take pleasure in the suffering of a creature of moral status, these pleasures should not count as part of the benefits of foxhunting. It is morally wrong to hunt foxes purely as a form of entertainment.

If there are no good reasons to kill foxes, foxhunting should be banned. But drag hunting could be encouraged instead. Of course, drag hunting could not have the history or incorporate all the traditions of foxhunting. But it would be possible for supporters of hunting to carry on customs similar to those that they wish to preserve.

The Benefits of Hunting: Jobs and the Environment

The *Burns Report* estimated that between 6,000 and 8,000 people depended on hunting for their livelihood, some directly employed by the hunts, others in businesses that supply the hunts but also do other work. When the hunt ban is enforced, some of these jobs will inevitably be lost. Some are very specialised to hunting, such as the kennelmen who look after the hounds, and it is unlikely that these people will find similar work.

The number of jobs involved in hunting is not large, however, compared with the number of jobs lost when other industries became obsolete: 36,000 jobs were lost in coal mining in the UK between 1980 and 2000, more than four times as many as are under threat from a hunt ban. In any case, if someone's job involves acting wrongly, they ought not to do it anyway; moreover, the government could support initiatives to help those who lose their jobs to find other work.

Defenders of foxhunting argue that it has had a beneficial effect on the environment. In recent decades, the size of farms has increased massively, and the hedgerows that used to divide smaller plots of land have been destroyed, endangering the wildlife that made their homes there. Huntsmen have managed the countryside to ensure that foxhunting continues, in particular by planting and maintaining woodland and hedges that provide cover for the fox. But foxhunts can cause conservation problems too, for instance during the hunt badgers and their setts are sometimes attacked by accident. Though hunts contributed to conserving the environment, there are many other ways of achieving this goal: the government could encourage farmers to protect hedgerows and promote biodiversity. The impact on the environment of the hunt ban need not be a problem.

Outlawing foxhunting is likely to lead to some job losses, and there could be a negative impact on the environment. But these costs have to be weighed against the reasons for supporting an outright ban.

The Law on Hunting

Foxhunts are seen by many as a pastime for a privileged few who trample on other people's land dressed in ridiculous costumes. If most people dislike foxhunts, and find the practice repellent, aren't we justified in passing a law that bans hunting?

The law should not be based on what a few people like or dislike. It should not even be decided by what the majority of people like or dislike. Even if most people could not bear the very thought of Mars bars deep-fried in batter, it should not be against the law to eat them. Whether people choose to eat Mars bars in batter is their own business.

Most people who oppose hunting do not just dislike hunting, as some people hate the idea of certain foods. They think that we ought not to hunt foxes, that people who join the hunt are morally bad. If most people agreed that foxhunting was morally bad, wouldn't we be justified in banning it?

Some things that are morally wrong are not matters for the law. Most people would agree that it is morally wrong to lie to your friends that you have forgotten your wallet when it is your round in the pub; but it is not against the law to do so, nor should it be. In the past, many people thought that homosexuality was morally wrong, but in the end they accepted that this was not a matter for legislation either.

Even if the majority of people in a society dislike some practice or think that it is morally wrong, it does not follow that we are justified in banning that practice. So are there any reasons for thinking that hunting should be banned?

Many of our laws, like the laws against theft and murder, are to prevent us from harming each other. If we were justified in making a law only to prevent harm to humans, there would be no grounds for a law against hunting: a ban would be an unwarranted restriction on the freedom of huntsmen.

We do, however, have laws whose purpose is to protect animals not humans. There are laws banning bear-baiting, cock-fighting and cruelty to animals. Animals that are capable of suffering have moral status: it matters morally when we make them suffer; it matters morally when we harm them. So it is appropriate to have laws that regulate the harm we may do to animals, just as it is right to have laws regulating harm to humans.

It is reasonable to ban foxhunting if foxhunting is cruel. Many people think that it must be, since its purpose is to chase down and kill an animal. But the defenders of hunting argue forcefully in response: killing foxes is necessary, for the sake of farm animals that foxes attack and for the sake of the fox population as a whole; trapping foxes is actually more cruel than hunting them, as the death of a fox in a hunt is swift whereas the death of a fox in a trap is often painfully prolonged. Whether or not we should ban foxhunting depends on these two issues: Are there good reasons to cull foxes? And does hunting cause foxes substantially more suffering than alternative methods of culling?

What Reasons Do We Have to Cull Foxes?

Hunt protestors argue that killing foxes is entirely unnecessary: foxhunting is gratuitous cruelty. They claim that hunters cause foxes to suffer for no purpose at all ... except their own pleasure.

Supporters of foxhunting reply that there are good reasons to cull foxes. They claim that those who are against hunting sentimentalise the fox, without being aware of the realities of life in the countryside: foxes kill other animals, including chickens and lambs belonging to farmers, and they spread disease. Not only are there good reasons to kill foxes on the basis of the welfare of other animals, there are even good reasons to cull the fox population for the sake of foxes themselves. Or so they claim.

Are foxes a significant threat to other animals? It is possible for them to transmit bacterial and viral diseases and parasites to pets and farm animals, though there is no clear evidence that they in fact regularly do so.

Many farmers believe that foxes attack their sheep and chickens. In places where lambs are born outdoors, it is estimated that 1 per cent of newborns are killed by foxes. Piglets are sometimes killed too if they are reared outside. Foxes will also attack poultry. These attacks can be devastating because the foxes do not limit themselves to killing what they can eat: they slaughter as many as they can. The vast majority of chickens are not at risk from foxes, though, because they are reared indoors in enormous factory farms that foxes cannot penetrate. Most vulnerable are those chickens reared in small free-range farms, which can lose more than 2 per cent of their birds.

Are farmers entitled to protect their livestock by killing foxes? Surely farmers could give extra protection to their own animals, for example by strengthening the fences that keep out predators, without actually killing anything.

Farmers should protect their animals in this way if they can. But it is not always practical to do so adequately when they are kept outdoors; it is not always possible to fence securely an entire field of sheep and lambs, for example. One solution would be to move all livestock that are at risk from foxes indoors, and rear no chickens, young sheep or pigs outside. But there are obvious welfare reasons not to farm these animals indoors. There are good reasons for farmers to insist on keeping their livestock outside; in which case it may not be practically possible to protect them adequately without killing foxes.

Hunt supporters argue that there are other reasons for culling the fox population too. A hunt selectively kills the weakest foxes, for weak and diseased foxes are typically the slowest and most likely to be caught by the hounds. As a result, the creatures that are left alive after a hunt are usually the strongest. Since it is these animals that go on to breed, producing the next generation of cubs, the population as a whole tends to become stronger. Hunting produces a population of fast, healthy and intelligent foxes. In addition, though it is by no means uncommon for species to be hunted to extinction, the fox population of the UK is not in immediate danger and huntsmen have powerful reasons to ensure that it never dies out; it is paradoxically true that so long as foxes are hunted, they will also be protected.

If the numbers of foxes were not managed through hunting and other kinds of selective cull, they would increase until there were too many foxes for their food supply. Then there would be a 'natural' reduction of fox numbers. In practice, this means that great numbers of foxes would die slowly and painfully from starvation or disease. If foxhunting were banned, we would condemn many foxes to an agonising death.

Defenders of foxhunting argue that we should consider the benefits of hunting to the *fox species as a whole*: the species is unlikely to die out, the population of foxes is likely to be healthier and stronger, and fewer foxes will die slowly of starvation. By contrast, critics of hunting emphasise that a foxhunt *deliberately* forces an *individual fox* to suffer pain and fear in the chase and the kill, and this is both unnecessary and unjustified.

When we consider our own species, we do not think that we are entitled to inflict suffering and death on an individual against their will for the benefit of the species: we would think it horrific if it were common practice to kill off the weakest human children. One element of the argument over foxhunting stems from a disagreement over whether benefits to the fox population can outweigh the cost to an individual fox, or whether, as in the case of humans, the individual has a trump card, the right to life.

There is a second crucial issue: given that we ought not to kill or harm animals ourselves, shouldn't we also try to *prevent* suffering in the animal world caused by others? If we ought not to kill but need not prevent suffering, we ought not to hunt foxes at all. On the other hand, if we should prevent animal suffering where we can, we *can* be justified in culling animals, either when a cull of a species benefits the animals of that species that are left alive, or when the culled animal inflicts suffering on other species.

In Chapter 9, it was argued that animals do not have the right to life. As a consequence, it may be right to kill one animal for the sake of saving other creatures from premature death. In at least some circumstances, killing foxes saves lambs, piglets and chickens from being killed, and saves other foxes from death by starvation: in those circumstances, killing foxes may be justified.

Although there are some circumstances in which killing foxes may be justified, this does not show that supporters of hunting were right all along. First, the hunts that took place may have been wholly unjustified: they may have killed foxes without benefiting other animals. Killing an animal can have far-reaching effects on the rest of the biological community – on other members of its species, on its predators, its prey and on their prey; effects that are very hard to predict. It is very difficult to know whether killing any animal will have good consequences, and in practice it may be exceptionally rare for killing foxes to be morally justified.

Second, even if a cull of foxes is permissible in some circumstances, foxhunting may still *not* be justified. There are several methods of killing foxes other than hunting them down with dogs: foxes could be trapped and slaughtered or shot instead. To see whether foxhunting is morally acceptable, we need to compare how much suffering each mode of culling involves. If foxhunting caused significantly more suffering than the alternatives, foxhunting would be morally wrong, even when killing foxes was justified.

How Much Suffering Does Hunting Cause?

It is difficult to tell how much an animal suffers: I might be able to imagine how I would feel if I were hunted by a pack of dogs, but I have no good reason to think that a fox would feel the same. We cannot try to work out how much suffering hunting causes by using our imagination. Instead, we need to find out in more detail what hunting involves, and how it affects a particular kind of animal. There has been a detailed study by the scientists Patrick Bateson and Elizabeth Bradshaw into deer hunting, but less work on foxhunting. Their study of deer hunting attempted to measure the effect of hunting on welfare, by estimating how much pain the deer had to endure as well as the 'stress' it suffered during the hunt.

In a deer hunt, the deer initially outruns the dogs easily, and sprints until it is far enough away from the hounds to feel safe, where it remains until the hounds get too near once more, and it sprints away again at top speed. The deer continues to make these swift sprints, until its muscles suffer glycogen depletion and it cannot run any further. It then turns to face the dogs at bay, making its last stand.

How much does the deer suffer during a hunt? Bateson and Bradshaw argue that in the past deer would have been hunted by wolves in short bursts, and so they have not evolved to cope with a long chase. They examined the bodies of hunted deer, and found that they contained very high levels of cortisol, a 'stress hormone', suggesting the deer had suffered from stress during the hunt. Their findings are disputed, because high levels of that hormone are also linked to exercise: humans who have run in a race often have high levels of cortisol too. But it is extremely likely that hunted deer do suffer from stress: the levels of cortisol are much higher than would be expected if the deer had merely been exercising.

If deer suffer stress during a hunt, isn't it obvious that foxes must do too? It does not necessarily follow that foxes suffer as deer do during the chase, for there may be significant differences in physiology between foxes and deer, and in any case the chase in a foxhunt is quite different from a deer hunt. A deer hunt consists in a series of sprints by the deer until it can run no more. The foxhunt is a continuous chase, typically lasting fifteen to twenty minutes, until the dogs overpower the fox. The fox is not chased until it cannot run any further. There is some evidence that the fox suffers physiological changes as a result of being chased that are most likely to be signs of stress, though again, they may merely be the result of vigorous exercise.

How much does a fox suffer during the kill? Supporters of foxhunting claim that the death is instantaneous and painless: a hound grabs the fox by the back of the neck and breaks its neck. There has not been an adequate survey of the injuries to hunted foxes to check whether this is true, but the evidence there is suggests that though hunted foxes may sometimes die instantly from a broken neck, they may instead be killed by massive damage to internal organs as they are attacked by the hounds. In either case, however, it is estimated that the fox will die within seconds; its death is certainly not prolonged, though it may be painful.

If the fox manages to escape from the hunt underground, it is 'dug out', that is, a terrier is sent down the hole to bring it out. This part of hunting almost certainly does cause significant injuries and stress to the fox, which is trapped in a confined space, and should probably be banned.

Alternatives to Hunting

Suppose that we accept the claims of hunt supporters that it is sometimes right to cull foxes. Hunting may still be morally unacceptable, if there are alternative methods of culling that cause less suffering than hunting. There are two main alternatives to hunting: trapping and shooting.

Traps or snares can be used to catch foxes so that they can be killed humanely. There are two main problems with snares from a welfare perspective. The first is that a fox that is caught round the neck does not wait calmly for someone to come along and put it out of its misery. Wild animals tend to suffer considerable stress when they are trapped and cannot escape. The second problem is that a trap will capture any suitably sized animal that is passing: about half the animals found in snares are not the intended victims. Of course, these animals can be released alive: trapping the wrong animal does not mean killing the wrong animal. But trapping inevitably means inflicting suffering on as many non-foxes as foxes. From a welfare perspective, trapping is arguably at least as bad as hunting, if not worse.

The main alternative to hunting animals is stalking and shooting them. If the marksman is accurate, shooting is a quick and painless death for an animal. The *Burns Report* argues that stalking and shooting deer is better from a welfare perspective, because it eliminates the need for the chase. The problem with shooting is that an inaccurate marksman can wound the animal rather than kill it. It is estimated that about 10 per cent of deer are killed using two or more shots, and that about 2 per cent of shot deer escape. A wounded animal can suffer greatly: it may die slowly from its wound in a few days or even longer, whereas a fox that is caught in a hunt dies very quickly, and a fox that is chased but escapes does not usually suffer significant injuries.

A fox is much smaller than a deer and therefore a more difficult target to hit. The most successful form of shooting foxes is known as lamping: the fox is caught in the beam of a high-powered spotlight and shot with a rifle. The *Burns Report* recommends lamping instead of hunting foxes, but recognises that it cannot be used in all circumstances. Because the spotlight is mounted on a vehicle, lamping is impossible on very hilly ground, and it is less successful in areas where there is good cover so that the fox can hide from the guns.

Should Foxhunting Have Been Banned?

Foxhunting for fun is morally unacceptable. We should hunt foxes only if we have good reasons to cull foxes and hunting is an acceptable method of culling.

Because the dispute over foxhunting is so heated, it is difficult to find reliable information about it. But there is some evidence that culling foxes has good welfare implications for their prey (especially chickens and lambs) and for the fox population as a whole. This suggests that culling foxes may be morally acceptable in at least a few circumstances.

If we do cull foxes, should we hunt them or use an alternative method? No method of culling is without negative implications for welfare. It is difficult to say how much suffering hunting causes: the actual kill is likely to be swift, but the fox may well suffer in the chase. The major alternative to hunting is shooting, which can kill foxes instantly, but can also merely wound them, causing them a painful prolonged death. It is likely that in terms of the welfare of the fox, shooting by a skilled marksman is the best method, but hunting may be more acceptable than shooting by an unskilled marksman who wounds rather than kills the animal. We need more information on the stress experienced by foxes in the chase to give a final verdict on the moral acceptability of foxhunting.

Should foxhunting be against the law? If we found out more about foxhunting, we might discover that the fox in the chase did not suffer much more than if it had exercised vigorously for half an hour, in which case there would not be grounds for a ban. Alternatively, we might discover that the suffering caused to the fox in the chase was unacceptable, in which case a ban would be appropriate. At the moment there is insufficient evidence to justify an outright ban.

Given this crucial lack of evidence, why did the British parliament make foxhunting illegal? Some of those who voted against foxhunting genuinely believed it to be cruel and barbaric. But some admitted that they were motivated mainly by class warfare: they were keen to outlaw a sport whose participants and supporters were mainly upper-class. Meanwhile, hunt supporters portrayed themselves as a downtrodden minority whose rights, freedoms and jobs were under threat from the tyranny of the majority. Despite the 700 hours of parliamentary time devoted to foxhunting, both sides managed to neglect what ought to have been the main issue: the effect of hunting on animal welfare. The evidence that we have suggests that many of the hunts that used to take place were probably unjustified. There was a great need for careful regulation of foxhunting to make sure that it occurred only where there were good reasons for culling foxes and where no better method of culling was available. But a total ban on the grounds of cruelty was not warranted.

CHAPTER THIRTEEN

SCIENCE AND SUFFERING

On 18 May 1984, five members of the Animal Liberation Front broke into the Head Trauma Research Centre at the University of Pennsylvania and stole about 30 videos made by members of the centre of their research on head injuries to baboons. When the tapes were shown in public, they shocked the whole of America.

The tapes showed baboons strapped into special helmets as a hydraulic piston hit the animal's head. The baboons suffered injuries similar to severe whiplash as the soft tissue of their brains moved inside their skulls, and ended up paralysed or comatose. The animals were supposed to be anaesthetised while these experiments took place but the anaesthetic used was inadequate and the baboons were sometimes conscious when the piston struck them. The researchers used instruments that were not properly cleaned, and could be seen laughing at the injured animals that were unable to move their limbs. The scientific justification for the experiments was wholly unclear; the researchers were investigating head injuries but they were not sure exactly what hypothesis they were trying to test.

The Research Centre was criticised for its procedures, but after some modifications, its funding was renewed.

Experimentation on Humans and Animals

Before the 19th century there were few experiments on animals or humans, but during that century doctors started to study medicine scientifically. They began to develop theories of various illnesses and how to cure them and to test these theories on both humans and animals. In America, new kinds of surgery were tried out on slaves with little concern for their suffering; scientists infected people with syphilis and gonorrhoea to study these diseases. After the Second World War, it was discovered that Nazi and Japanese scientists had conducted horrific experiments on their prisoners of war. They deliberately infected prisoners with malaria, typhus and jaundice, tried out different kinds of poison, and experimented with methods of sterilising men and women. Many prisoners died after terrible suffering.

Twenty-three Germans were tried for war crimes involving scientific experiments; sixteen were found guilty. In their defence, the scientists and doctors argued that in order to gain significant medical advances, they were justified in inflicting suffering on a few people, and claimed, as was almost certainly true, that there were many precedents in the past of medical experiments being carried out without the consent of the subjects. In response, the Nuremberg Court set out the 'Nuremberg Code', ten elements needed to justify a medical experiment on humans that included: the experiment should lead to an important result, it should be properly designed, similar experiments on animals should previously have been carried out, it should be conducted by properly qualified scientists, and any human subject should have voluntarily consented to the experiment.

The Nuremberg Code restricted experimentation on humans severely by requiring that all human subjects give their consent, ruling out any experiments on humans who could not give consent – the unconscious, the mentally disabled, and the very young – but of course permitted experiments on animals (in fact, it went so far as to require experimentation on animals prior to experimentation on humans). But the Nuremberg Code was deemed to be too demanding by the medical profession, who preferred to adopt the 'Helsinki Declaration', set out by the World Medical Association in 1964. The Helsinki Declaration requires only that any human involved in an experiment should have given their voluntary consent to their involvement, *if they are capable of giving their consent*. If they are unable to consent, consent is not required.

It is estimated that over 41 million animals are used in experiments each year worldwide. The experiments range from basic research into biology, physiology and psychology, to research into the diagnosis, treatment and prevention of disease, from the testing of consumer products for safety, to the training of students in dissection. A huge variety of animals are used, including mice, rats, rabbits, pigs and primates, sometimes bred as laboratory animals, sometimes captured from the wild. In 1876, the UK became the first country to pass legislation controlling animal experiments, and British law is currently among the most demanding in the world. In the UK, scientists have to be licensed to carry out experiments on animals and their research has to be monitored by qualified inspectors. The suffering of the animals in the experiments is ranked as mild, moderate or severe, where the last might include severe trauma and death. The more serious the suffering of the animal, the more significant and worthy the outcome of the experiment must be if it is to go ahead. The experiment will not be permitted if there are alternatives that would inflict less suffering on animals, or that do not involve animals at all. A handful of other countries have followed in legally requiring certain standards in animal experimentation, a few more have a code of practice, but many countries have no laws at all governing animal research.

Experiments and Voluntary Consent

Many scientists used to think that science was value-neutral. They believed that though their research might be used in morally problematic ways, as when their understanding of the fundamental nature of the atom was used in developing nuclear weapons, the research itself raised no awkward ethical questions. The Nazi experiments on humans show beyond any doubt that they were mistaken: *scientific research itself can be morally wrong*. Even if the Nazi experiments had given us useful information about diseases like malaria and possible treatments of them, it was wrong for those scientists deliberately to infect humans with diseases without their consent.

It is often thought that doctors should make sure that their human patients voluntarily consent to every medical procedure before it is carried out on them. In practice, this is often impossible: the patient may be too sick to give his or her consent or may even be unconscious. If the doctor is about to give the patient a therapeutic treatment, that is, a procedure in the patient's best interests, it is usually acceptable for the doctor to continue without the patient's consent, particularly if the patient's relatives have been consulted.

Animals cannot give their voluntary consent to any scientific or medical procedure. No scientist could explain to the animal what it involved or why it was necessary; even if an animal could grasp the point of a treatment, it could not reflect on the reasons for and against it and come to a reasoned decision. Of course, you could open up the doors to the cages of animals in laboratories to see if the animals would run away. But you could not interpret the animal staying in its cage as consent to continue with the treatment, for the animal might be conditioned into dependence on its familiar surroundings. Nor could you take the animal's leaving as a sign that it had made a decision not to continue the experiment: it might have been moved by a mere instinct, perhaps an instinct to avoid a confined space.

Some medical treatments of animals are therapeutic; vets often operate on animals in the best interests of the animal.

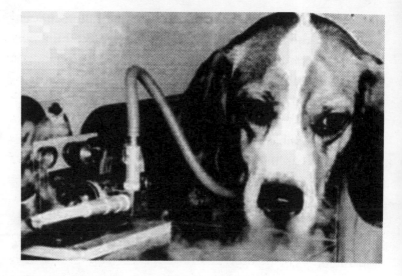

An experiment to test the effects of smoking

It is clearly ethically acceptable for a vet to treat the animal in its own interests – to operate on the broken leg of a dog or cat, for example – even though the animal did not, and could not, give its consent to the treatment. But most scientific research on animals is non-therapeutic: the beneficiaries of the research are usually human.

In a non-therapeutic experiment on humans, one human is harmed and perhaps killed for the sake of benefiting others. It is generally accepted that for humans who can give consent, such an experiment is justified *only* if the benefits sufficiently outweigh the harms, *and* the human to be harmed has given his or her consent. Why is consent important here? One possibility is that we are not justified in harming one person for the sake of others, even when the benefits to them are enormous (suppose that you could develop a drug to save thousands of people from malaria by deliberately infecting one person with the disease), because it is wrong to use one person for the sake of others. But if the patient consents to the experiment, even though they are still harmed in order to benefit others, we are no longer using them unjustly: the experiment can go ahead.

According to this conception of the importance of consent, non-therapeutic experiments are not justified unless one has the patient's consent, because in any non-therapeutic experiment the patient is harmed for the sake of others. The Nuremberg Code endorses this conception of consent by requiring that no experiment on a human should *ever* take place without his or her consent, whether or not he or she is autonomous and so capable of making such a judgement.

Despite the fact that the Nuremberg Code permits experiments on animals, if we accept the view of the importance of consent that the Code endorses, it is hard to see how any non-therapeutic experiments on animals could be justified. If it is wrong to use humans who are not autonomous by harming them for the sake of others, surely it must also be wrong to use animals that are not autonomous in the same way. However much we might benefit from research on animals, all such experiments must be illegitimate.

On the other hand, consent might be important in quite a different way. It may be acceptable to use one person for the sake of others provided that the benefits are sufficiently great, but unjust to disregard the consent of the people involved. The Nazi and Japanese doctors may be wrong, not because they harmed prisoners for the sake of others, but because they did so in ways to which the prisoners did not consent. These prisoners were certainly capable of giving or withholding their consent to the medical experiments to which they were subjected, but they were not given a chance to refuse, and their objections were ignored. On this view, it is not necessarily wrong to perform a non-therapeutic experiment on a person; it is wrong to do so if they have refused to participate, or if you have not allowed them to decide whether they want to do so.

On this alternative model of the significance of consent, if a human has not been and never will be capable of giving his or her consent to a non-therapeutic experiment, it may sometimes be acceptable to carry out the experiment nonetheless if the benefits for others are great. The Helsinki Declaration endorses this conception of consent because it permits experiments on humans who are not autonomous. If this conception of consent is right, experiments on animals can be justified if the benefits are sufficient, even though animals cannot give their consent.

Whether or not we ought to experiment on animals depends on which conception of consent is correct. Though this is a controversial matter, it seems to me that we ought to accept the conception endorsed by the Helsinki Declaration. There is an important moral difference between harming David, a normal human, without his consent, and harming Fido, a normal dog. When you harm David without his consent, you refuse to accept that what he chooses for himself matters. You fail to treat with respect his own judgements about his own life. When you harm Fido without his consent, you cannot be ignoring his own choice about his life, you cannot be failing to respect his judgement, because he cannot make any reasoned choices or judgements at all.

Of course, just because an experiment *might* produce some benefits for us, this certainly does *not* mean that the experiment is justified. There are many other reasons why an experiment might be wrong: it may be wrong to perform an experiment on a human who is incapable of consent without gaining the consent of his or her near relatives. Many experiments on animals may be prohibited because the suffering imposed on the animal would be too great, and the expected benefits of the experiment do not sufficiently outweigh that pain and distress. For example, the experiments performed on baboons at the Head Trauma Research Centre at the University of Pennsylvania appear to be wholly unjustified, because significant harms were inflicted on the animals without clear benefits in terms of improved scientific or medical understanding. The Helsinki Declaration implies that *some* experiments on animals may be acceptable; many such experiments may be totally wrong.

What Kinds of Experiments on Animals Are Justified?

There are at least three different reasons for experimenting on animals:

1. For educational purposes, for example for dissection and practising surgery.
2. To test consumer goods for safety.
3. To contribute to basic research in biology, physiology and psychology (for example about the nature of the brain), and to biological research about the nature of diseases and the development of treatments (for example research into Alzheimer's disease and potential treatments).

Some of these uses of animals are easier to justify than others, because their benefits are more significant.

Dissection in Education

Dissection used to be a standard part of the school biology curriculum, especially in America where an estimated 3 million frogs a year were dissected by schoolchildren and it was not uncommon for a student to have dissected a frog, a foetal pig, a cat and a dog before leaving school. Frogs are becoming an endangered species in the USA as a result, and there is really no need for schoolchildren to dismember animals at all. Students of biology can learn anatomy from textbooks and computer simulations of dissection instead. Since there is little educational benefit in most dissections of animals in schools, but the harm to animals, which must be killed, is considerable, the practice should not continue except in the case of university students training to be vets or researchers who need to be skilled at dissection.

Safety Tests for Consumer Goods

European legislation requires that the ingredients of consumer products from washing powder and washing-up liquid to lipsticks, shampoo and sunblock are tested on animals for safety. These tests protect the customers who use the product and the chemists who manufacture it from injury, and also help to protect the environment from pollution. Though some well-known companies advertise that they do not test products on animals, many of the ingredients of their products have been tested on animals at some time for some purpose.

Some of the safety tests on animals have become notorious after campaigns by animal rights protestors. The Draize eye test involved putting a diluted solution of the test substance into the eyes of six rabbits. The rabbits' eyes were observed for three days for signs of irritation and any damage was monitored for a further three weeks to see whether or not the eye repaired itself. In early forms of the Draize test, the rabbits' heads were clamped into position so that they could not touch their eye and they were caused considerable pain and sometimes blinded. The test is now modified to cause them less pain: the rabbits may be free to move about and anaesthetic may be used. In addition, significantly fewer Draize tests are now carried out: the test is not performed on substances that we already know to be irritants, such as strongly acidic or alkaline substances and those that on previous tests were shown to irritate. But nevertheless there remain serious questions over the Draize test, in particular over whether its results are relevant to humans at all. The rabbit eye is significantly different from the human eye: unlike humans, the rabbit has a third eyelid and rabbits produce fewer tears than humans. But there is no accepted alternative to the test, and it is still used in its modified form.

The LD50 test for toxicity was used to determine how much of a given product could be ingested by rats until half of the test population of 60 to 80 rats died. In other words, every time the test was carried out, at least 30 rats had to lose their lives. Sometimes the quantity of the test substance needed to kill 30 rats was far beyond the amount that any human might ingest. The LD50 test is no longer commonly used; instead, where possible, scientists estimate the toxicity of substances based on the known toxicity of similar chemicals. When new substances have to be tested, the test has been modified so that fewer rats are used and it is no longer essential for any of them to die during the experiment: typically about twenty rats are given a specific quantity of the test substance; if the rats are unharmed, it is considered non-toxic; further tests are made only if two or more rats die.

The most notorious animal tests of the past have been modified to reduce animal suffering and to restrict the number of animals dying during the test. But should we test these consumer products on animals at all? Of course, it would be wrong to allow untested, potentially dangerous chemicals, cosmetics and household cleaners to be sold to the public. But we could instead simply refuse to allow new products containing untested chemicals to be sold; after all, we have a lot of consumer goods already.

Many people think that animal testing of cosmetics and other consumer products should be banned, because though new products make our lives somewhat more pleasant, they could not be said to give us significant benefits that out-weigh the harm we inflict on animals in testing their safety. If the safety tests could be modified further so that animals barely suffered during them, it is possible that the pleasure we gained from our new consumer goods would outweigh the harm inflicted, and it would be acceptable to test these products on animals. But though it is very difficult to weigh human pleasures against animal suffering, it seems likely that often the animal suffering outweighs the benefits to us,

Rabbits testing the safety of cosmetics

and so in most cases new consumer products should be tested using alternatives to animal testing, or should not be released at all.

Scientific and Medical Experiments

Many people think that if we can cure human diseases with drugs that we have researched and developed through testing on animals, there need be no further argument: if we could find a cure for cancer by research on animals, we ought to go ahead, it's just obvious that such experiments would be justified. But things are not so simple.

First, it is rare for scientists to *know* that the outcome of a course of experiments will be so successful. They might discover a new wonder drug that cures cancer; they might find that their drug is only partially successful, that it has terrible side effects, or that it does not work at all. When a scientist begins her research, she cannot be certain what the benefits of the research will be, or even if there will be any benefits; whereas she knows for sure that she will inflict suffering on some animals.

Second, even if the research does produce a new wonder drug, it is not obvious that it should take place. The Nazi research on humans could have produced a significant medical breakthrough, but their means, deliberately infecting prisoners with malaria and other diseases, did not justify their end.

Third, some medical and scientific experiments on animals are not intended to produce new drugs that will improve the health of future generations of mankind. They are intended to give us knowledge, a better understanding of the physiology and psychology of animals and hopefully of ourselves too. Sometimes basic understanding of biology and physiology can turn out to be crucial in combating disease, sometimes it has no immediate practical applications, and sometimes it is never of any practical use. Scientific knowledge can be worth having for its own sake. It is important for us to understand our own bodies and minds and the animals around us if we can. But is the value of scientific knowledge so great that it is worth causing suffering to animals to gain that knowledge? When scientists want to experiment on animals to find a cure for a disease such as Alzheimer's, we can compare the harms imposed on the animals during the experiment with the suffering we will prevent if we can cure that disease. Of course it is very difficult to weigh up these harms and benefits, but there are at least some similarities between the harms we cause in the experiment and those we avert. By contrast, when we experiment to gain scientific knowledge that has no immediate application, we have to weigh up very different things: the harm of suffering compared with the value of scientific understanding. Because this comparison is so difficult to make, it is much harder to decide whether animal experiments are justified when the goal is knowledge rather than a useful drug. Certainly many animal experiments would be totally unjustified, because the value of the understanding we would gain by performing the experiment would not outweigh the harm to the animal, but at least some experiments on animals to gain pure knowledge, without practical applications, may be acceptable.

Fourth, it is not always possible to apply results about animal biology, physiology and disease to humans. There are obvious differences between humans and rabbits, rats and even primates. Sometimes a drug that has no side effects on humans is dangerous to animals: aspirin causes birth defects in monkeys but not in humans. Some drugs have no side effects on animals but can be deadly to humans: carbenoxalone, a drug used to treat gastric ulcers, has no dangerous effects on monkeys but can cause heart failure in humans. The notorious drug thalidomide was tested extensively on animals and found to be harmless before it was released for sale, but caused appalling birth defects when taken by pregnant women. In fact, thalidomide has very variable results in different species: it can cause birth defects in humans and in certain kinds of rabbits and primates, but not in rats, mice, guinea pigs and other primates. Testing Aids drugs on chimpanzees turned out to be of little benefit, as chimps infected with the HIV virus, unlike humans, rarely develop full-blown Aids. There is no guarantee that animal experiments will be of any benefit to us at all.

Citing these and other examples, some animal rights protestors argue that experiments on animals should be banned because they are worthless, never contributing to useful medical research or to the development of successful drugs and vaccines. In fact, they say, animal testing can actually make us worse off, because we end up using drugs like thalidomide, thinking they are safe when they are not. The protestors are correct that it is not always possible to apply the results of tests on animals to humans. But their claims that tests on animals are never useful or that experiments on animals never contribute to medical advances are simply false. For example, in 1922, Banting and Best discovered insulin and showed that it could be used to treat diabetes by experimenting on dogs and rabbits. Their discovery saved millions of people's lives.

In January 2004, vigorous protests by anti-vivisectionists contributed to the decision of Cambridge University not to build a neuroscience laboratory that would have investigated brain disorders including Parkinson's disease and Alzheimer's. The costs of the laboratory had risen sharply, partly in order to provide adequate security for the scientists and staff to protect them from the animal activists. The Cambridge scientists had intended to conduct experiments on primates, the animals that are most closely related to us, because primate brains are most similar to ours, but their use is extremely controversial for precisely this reason.

Scientists who are involved in such research face a dilemma. In some experiments, less developed animals that may not even be able to feel pain, such as invertebrates, may be used, but for research into diseases of the brain, it is important that the animals tested are much more similar to us. The most useful experiments, whose results are most likely to apply to humans, are those performed on other humans and on primates. But the more closely related the animals are to humans, the more ethical questions the experiments raise: it is harder to justify experimenting on an animal for our benefit when we know that it is both sensitive and psychologically complex. If possible, scientists should avoid experimenting on primates and research brain disorders in different ways, for example by using brain-imaging scans on humans who suffer from the disease. Some animal rights activists want experiments on primates completely outlawed. Such a ban might be warranted if primates were autonomous, that is, if they, like humans, were capable of making reasoned judgements about their own life. The evidence that we have is that though primates have more sophisticated minds than nearly any other non-human animal, they are not autonomous. If research on primates could bring us great benefits that we could not achieve in any other way, those experiments might be justified. Primate research should not be banned, but it is morally acceptable in very few circumstances.

When Is Animal Research Justified?

We ought not to make animals suffer unnecessarily, but the benefits of scientific research can be considerable, and can warrant experimenting on animals. Scientific research on animals should not be prohibited altogether, but it should be very carefully regulated, to ensure that scientists carry out experiments only when the expected outcomes are sufficiently worthwhile and that they avoid causing unnecessary suffering. Animal activists are right to campaign to ensure that appropriate animal welfare regulations are enforced, though it is quite wrong for them to do so by threatening violence to scientists and laboratory staff.

Scientists should use specially bred laboratory animals where possible rather than animals brought in from the wild, because wild animals suffer severe trauma when they are captured, transported and kept in captivity. Lab animals should be housed in an appropriate environment, and be properly fed and watered; if possible, social animals should not be kept in isolation. The suffering imposed by any given experiment should be kept to a minimum; anaesthetics should be used to reduce distress whenever doing so does not interfere with the research. The experiment must be carefully assessed before it begins to determine what suffering the animal is likely to undergo, what the potential benefits are, and whether they are worth the harm inflicted on the animal. As part of this assessment, the scientist and his or her research committee need to consider whether there is any equally valid method of experimentation that would impose less suffering on the animals, that would require fewer animals to be harmed or that would involve less developed animals (for example invertebrates rather than vertebrates). Finally they need to consider whether it is essential to experiment on animals at all: some animal experiments can be replaced by *in vitro* experiments on cells or organs and sometimes computer simulations can be used instead.

Scientists who experiment on animals should obey the 'three Rs':

- *Refinement*: the experiment must be designed so that the animal suffers as little as possible.
- *Reduction*: as few animals as possible should be used in the experiment, and the animals used must be of as low psychological development as possible.
- *Replacement*: computer simulations, mathematical models and *in vitro* experiments must replace experiments on animals wherever possible.

Animal rights activists claim that all experiments on animals could be replaced. They are right to point out that it is increasingly possible for scientists to use other kinds of model in their research. But it seems unlikely that in the future all experiments on animals will be worthless, and we should not rule out such research when its outcomes can be immensely valuable. Scientific experiments on animals should not be banned, but must be carefully regulated.

CHAPTER FOURTEEN

MAN'S BEST FRIEND?

Odysseus, king of Ithaca, left his home and family to fight in the Trojan War. The war lasted for ten years, but Odysseus's troubles had barely started. As he tried to return to Ithaca, he encountered a series of terrible obstacles: the fearsome one-eyed Cyclops; the Sirens who lure men to their death; Scylla the monster and Charybdis the giant whirlpool; and many more. Odysseus finally reached home twenty years after he had left. Returning in disguise, the king was recognised by no one, until he came across Argos, a dog he himself had trained before sailing for Troy. Argos was old and sick but wagged his tail and tried to summon the strength to crawl up to him. Odysseus wiped away a tear as his dog, having seen his master one last time, lay down to die.

Homer's *Odyssey* describes a memorable emotional bond between a man and his dog, who know each other and care for each other even though they have been parted for many years. Similarly, in *The Call of the Wild*, Jack London portrays a fierce love between Buck and John Thornton that leads the dog many times to risk his life to save the man.

Although many books on animal ethics discuss hunting, eating animals and experimenting on them, few devote attention to pets. This is surprising because the relationship between a pet and its owner clearly has a moral dimension. Many people become extremely fond of their pets, lavishing attention on them, feeding and looking after them extremely well. They treat their pets far better than other animals. When people treat their pets badly, neglecting or abandoning them, even deliberately harming them, it is natural to think that these people have done something worse than when they neglect animals that are not their pets; most of us think not just that pet-owners may give special consideration to their pets, but that they ought to do so.

Pets are companion animals; they are quite different from wild animals that are not domesticated, that cannot live among human beings but can survive on their own: most pets could not live without our assistance. Perhaps this reliance of pets on humans generates a special relationship between humans and animals.

The philosopher Roger Scruton is sceptical that animals have rights in general, but makes an exception for pets, which he thinks of as 'honorary members of our moral community'. We have special responsibilities to pets, he argues in his book *Animal Rights and Wrongs*, because we made our pets *dependent* on us by leading them to *expect* that we would look after their needs.

Is the basis of our obligations to our pets their expectations that we will treat them in a certain way? It is very hard to believe that our obligations can be explained in this way:

in the first place, a pet would have to have beliefs about what will happen to it in the future, whereas it is very controversial whether any animals can think about the future at all; second, many owners feel that they ought to give their pets medicine when they are ill, but it is obvious that most animals have no beliefs at all about what medicine they ought to take. And even when animals do clearly form expectations about how we will treat them, we do not always have obligations towards them. Imagine that I spill some caviar outside my house, and a stray cat that eats it forms the expectation that I will give it the same treat every day. It is obvious that I have no obligation to give the cat caviar. So Scruton must be mistaken: we do not owe to our pets whatever they expect us to provide for them.

Friendship

Many people think of their pet, especially a pet dog, as their friend. Others are sceptical about this claim: surely people who think that they have a meaningful relationship with an animal are foolishly anthropomorphic and sadly deluded. Is it ridiculous to think that you could be friends with your pet?

The ancient Greek philosopher Aristotle describes friendships as relationships that involve mutual good will; different kinds of friendship depend on diverse reasons for wishing your friend well. Some friendships are based on pleasure and depend on the friends enjoying each other's company and taking pleasure in shared activities. If the friendship is genuine, we will be happy when our friends are happy or successful; we will sympathise when our friends are upset or unhappy. Other friendships are deeper and more important than friendships of pleasure: Aristotle calls these *moral friendships*. Moral friends trust one another with their most personal confessions and problems; they confide in each other, ask for advice about what to do, and offer advice when requested. We rely on our moral friends and trust them, sharing our thoughts and feelings with them. We know that our moral friends rely on us too, and we try to be worthy of their trust.

Moral friends whom we can confide in and who give us good advice may be our best friends, but friendships of pleasure are still genuine friendships that are both valuable and important to us. Both kinds of friendship can make our lives happier. We care more for our friends and treat them better than other people, but we are entitled to do so (within limits) because our lives would be so much more boring and miserable without friends.

Can we have friendships with animals? It is unlikely that we could have this kind of relationship with a stick insect or a goldfish. But we may be able to have friendships with some animals, such as dogs. There are many popular stories of special relationships between dogs and humans, from Odysseus's dog Argos, to Buck and, best known of all, Lassie, who always came back home to her family.

Many people who have dogs are very close to their pets. They care about their dog for the animal's own sake. They buy the right sort of food for it, make sure it is regularly fed, and if it is sick, they get advice from a vet and nurse it back to health. They know that their pet is a long-term commitment; they expect to live with it until the dog dies or becomes very ill. They are usually the best-placed people to notice if there is something the matter with their dog, because they know their own pet so well; they are unhappy if their dog is miserable.

At least some owners have the right kind of attitudes towards their dogs for their relationship to count as a kind of friendship: they care for Rover for his own sake, enjoy his company, and are happy when he is happy.

Does Rover have good will towards his owner? Some dogs seem to be able to tell the difference between their owners and other people: they are less likely to bark at or bite their owners and more likely to expect food from them and to be taken for a walk. This tendency can be accentuated through training: a dog can be taught to come to his owner when called, and to obey other simple commands. Of course, these dogs may simply have been conditioned with rewards or the prospect of food to be nice towards their owners, but it is not out of the question that they are responding with good will to the good will that their owners show to them, as Buck and Argos do, even if they do not consciously recognise it as such. If so, dogs *can* be friends with their owners.

What kind of friendship can we expect between dogs and humans? An ideal dog–owner relationship is typically pleasant for the owner and dog; both enjoy the other's company and their shared activities. Dogs and humans can have friendships of pleasure, but it is much more difficult to believe that they can have a moral friendship, based around mutual confidences, the exchange of feelings and of judgements, and the giving and receiving of advice. You can tell a dog your most intimate confidences, but he will not understand what you are saying to him; he will never be able to judge whether what you did was right or wrong, or whether or not you should feel guilty; nor can he tell you his confidences in return. Dogs cannot be our moral friends because they cannot understand morally complex human situations; they could not give advice or help us to work out what to do, even if they could communicate with us.

Dogs are sometimes thought of as particularly loyal companions, as 'man's best friend'. This is a mistake. Although they could not have the flaws that might prevent a human from becoming a moral friend – they are not disloyal, they do not betray you or lead you into wrong-doing with their bad advice – nor are they capable of the virtues that your best friends ought to have – they cannot share your most private thoughts and worries. They do not *choose* to be loyal; they can never lead you towards doing the right thing with their good advice.

We can enjoy pleasurable and useful friendships with our pets. If you decide to take on a dog, you should look after him, ensure that he is well fed and healthy and train him to be domesticated so that you can live with him. You should take on hobbies – going for walks, playing with sticks – that you can share with the dog, to develop your friendship with him.

We are justified in treating our human friends of pleasure better than strangers because pleasant friendships are valuable. A special concern for one's dog is justified in the same way: we are right to treat our pets better than we treat other animals because we have worthwhile relationships with our pets, which we can nurture and develop by treating our pets well.

Because you live closely with your pet, you are particularly well placed to know what it needs. Ignoring those needs would be callous; only if you were exceptionally obtuse could you remain unaware of them. It is more understandable to neglect the needs of animals that are not right in front of you. In addition, if you mistreat your pet, using your dog to take out your frustrations, kicking and shouting at it for fun, you are exploiting the fact that it lives with you and is almost entirely dependent on you to treat it cruelly. In hurting your dog, you are subverting what ought to be a valuable relationship in order to do harm. So it is usually worse to mistreat your pet than to neglect or harm other animals.

Once we understand the ways in which dogs can be friends with us, we can explain why we ought to give extra attention to our pets. But at the same time we need to acknowledge that there is an important moral difference between dogs and humans, as we cannot share the most valuable kinds of relationship, moral friendships, with dogs or other animals. Pet–owner relationships cannot be as important as human friendships and it would be a mistake to devote one's life to animals at the expense of developing long-lasting, intimate human relationships that have at least the potential to be more worthwhile.

The nature of friendship with dogs shows that there are morally significant qualities of animals that are not directly connected to sentience or intelligence. Many wild animals respond to us too defensively or aggressively for us to be able to develop valuable relationships with them. Wolves may be as intelligent as dogs and as sensitive, but their emotions and their responses to emotions in us are simply incompatible with human social life; we cannot develop friendships with them. As a consequence, we may be justified in treating dogs better than wolves even though both species are equally sensitive to pain and equally intelligent. We may even be justified in treating dogs better than equally sensitive and *more* intelligent wild animals, such as chimpanzees, for it is hard for us to develop friendships with chimps, but we can be friends with dogs.

CHAPTER FIFTEEN

CONCLUSION: MORE EQUAL THAN OTHERS

After the revolution that left them managing Animal Farm, the animals all agreed to live by a set of seven rules. When Napoleon and his porcine lieutenants took over the farm, they changed the final commandment from:

> All animals are equal

to the rather less perspicuous:

> All animals are equal, but some animals are more equal than others.

While it does not strictly make sense to say that anything is 'more equal' than anything else, it is easy enough to grasp what the pigs were trying to express: that they were the superiors of the other animals. According to Orwell, believing oneself to be more valuable than others is a distinctively human characteristic, for it is when the pigs make this claim that they finally become indistinguishable from men.

Orwell is right that some humans think they are better than other creatures and that they are entitled to treat nature as their dominion. On the other hand, there are animal rights activists who accept *Animal Farm*'s seventh commandment in its original form: they think it obvious that all animals are equal. Both these views are too extreme, and both are too simplistic.

Any animal that can suffer has moral status: it matters morally when it is harmed. In this respect all sentient animals are genuine equals. It is therefore wrong to treat animals cruelly. It is wrong to make them suffer for our entertainment. It is wrong to kill them for trivial reasons. We do not have dominion over the natural world.

But in other ways animals are not equal. They have very different mental capacities. Some animals probably cannot feel even simple emotions like fear and anxiety; some are not capable of simple reasoning to help them get what they want; some are not able to think about the future and make plans about it; some have no idea about other creatures' minds.

Because they have more developed minds, some animals can enjoy more sophisticated kinds of goods than others. If they die prematurely, they are deprived of these goods. So it is, for instance, typically worse for a human to die than a great ape, but it is also worse for a great ape to die than an insect.

We know that there are moral limits to our treatment of animals; and we know that these are not the same as the moral limits to our treatment of humans. But what should be our relationship to the rest of the natural world?

Should we try to efface ourselves entirely, withdrawing until we have a minimal impact on the natural world? This goal of the 'invisible man' is plainly unrealistic. The natural world is where we live; we are part of it and we cannot avoid affecting it.

Should we try to supervise nature, minimising suffering and preventing animals from killing one another? While the role of 'invisible man' calls for too little intervention in the natural world, the role of 'policeman' calls for far too much. It would be immensely demanding to have to be for ever improving nests, burrows and warrens and making pigeons, rats and badgers more comfortable. And there are enormously complicated connections between different species, so that any intervention we made to benefit some animals could have a huge negative impact on other creatures, an effect that we simply could not predict.

We need to find a way to live with animals, taking account of the benefits and costs to them as well as to ourselves. But once we see that animals have moral status, but are not in all respects equal to one another, we find that it is exceptionally difficult to balance their interests with ours.

It is clear that for too long we have weighted the scales enormously on our own side, allowing great harm to animals for the sake of small benefits to us, factory farming being an obvious, and indefensible, example. Animal welfare activists have campaigned long and hard to alter this mindset. They have met with considerable success, raising awareness of the plight of the worst-treated animals, and producing steady, if slow, change. There is a general acknowledgement that the number of scientific experiments on animals should be reduced. The living conditions of livestock on the farm and creatures in the laboratory have gradually improved, though much remains to be done.

The excellent work of activists who campaign for stricter animal welfare laws, and for proper enforcement of current laws, should ensure that this progress continues. It is important, however, that their protests take place within the law. Threatening violence towards people who are thought to be guilty of cruelty towards animals is completely wrong. As most activists know, acceptance of the moral status of animals will not be encouraged by failures to respect the moral status of humans.

Should animal activists aim to end scientific experimentation on animals, to ban hunting and farming? Many activists obviously do regard these as their goals. But as we have seen, each of these issues is extremely complex.

Foxhunting is a good example of this. Many protestors see foxhunting as a paradigm of unjustified cruelty that obviously should be banned. But we find that there are good reasons for us to manage the fox population, and foxhunting may be a legitimate way of doing so. While there are excellent grounds for strict and carefully enforced regulation of hunting, it is not at all clear that an outright ban is justified.

Similarly, many animal activists think that scientific experiments on animals are never justified. But though there is a constant danger that scientists fail to weigh the interests of animals against their desire to make progress or to test their pet theory, improvements in scientific understanding and in medicine can justify animal experimentation. We need very powerful reasons to justify experimenting on animals, but sometimes we do have such reasons.

Perhaps the hardest questions of all are about eating animals. While some kinds of farming plainly cause a great deal of suffering, animals can benefit as well as be harmed by farming, and it is hard to say where the balance of reasons lies here. At the least, though, it is not absolutely clear that all farming is wrong and that no one should eat meat. In general, animal activists should campaign for better treatment of animals within these familiar practices, rather than trying to end them altogether.

Though, like other animals, we are part of the natural world, we humans are nevertheless unique within it. We are the only creatures that are morally responsible for our actions. This is a great benefit to us: the same capacities that enable us to be morally responsible are also, in part, the grounds of our right to life. But moral responsibility is also a burden: it compels us to think very hard about our relationship with the rest of nature, and especially our treatment of other creatures with moral status. None of these issues is easy to resolve, but they present a challenge we cannot refuse: striving to find the answers is part of what it is to be human.

FURTHER READING

Chapter 2: Animal Rights Through the Ages
The views in the ancient world about animals are described by
Richard Sorabji, *Animal Minds and Human Morals* (Ithaca:
Cornell University Press, 1993). A Christian perspective,
sympathetic to animal rights, can be found in Andrew Linzey,
Animal Rights (London: SCM Press, 1976), while details of
Buddhist views on animals are given in Chapter 4 of Peter
Harvey, *An Introduction to Buddhist Ethics* (Cambridge:
Cambridge University Press, 2000).
Charles Darwin's theories can be found in his great works, *The
Origin of Species* (London: Murray, 1859) and *The Descent of
Man* (London: Murray, 1871).
The changes to the UK law on animals are explained in Mike
Radford, *Animal Welfare Law in Britain* (Oxford: Oxford
University Press, 2001).
Peter Singer has written a large number of books, many of which
outline his views on life, death, rights, and the ethical treat-
ment of humans and animals. He wrote probably the most
influential defence of the moral status of animals, *Animal
Liberation* (New York: Random House, 1975; London:
Pimlico, 1995). His philosophical views can be found in more
detail in *Practical Ethics* (Cambridge: Cambridge University
Press, 1993), which also defends the moral significance of

animals. His views are discussed in *Singer and His Critics*, edited by Dale Jamieson (Oxford: Blackwell's, 1999).

The quote from Jeremy Bentham is taken from his *Introduction to the Principles of Morals and Legislation* (1789; Oxford: Clarendon Press, 1995).

Chapter 3: Can They Suffer?

The quote from Descartes' contemporary is reported by Peter Singer, *Animal Liberation*, p. 201.

Excellent, scientifically informed accounts of the evidence that animals are conscious and feel pain are found in Bernard Rollin, *The Unheeded Cry* (Oxford: Oxford University Press, 1989), especially pp. 97–129, 137–61; and David Degrazia, *Taking Animals Seriously* (Cambridge: Cambridge University Press, 1996), Chapter 5.

A seminal article on the problems in knowing what other creatures experience is Thomas Nagel's 'What Is It Like to Be a Bat?', reprinted in his *Mortal Questions* (Cambridge: Cambridge University Press, 1979).

More sceptical about animal minds are Dan Dennett, *Kinds of Mind* (New York: Phoenix, 1997), Chapters 3 and 6; and Peter Carruthers, *The Animals Issue* (Cambridge: Cambridge University Press, 1992), Chapter 8.

Kenneth Grahame's wildly anthropomorphic novel *The Wind in the Willows* (Oxford: Oxford World's Classics, 1999) was first published in 1908.

Chapter 4: Can They Reason?

There are some extremely interesting books written by animal experts, including Marc Hauser, *Wild Minds* (New York: Henry Holt, 2000), and numerous works by Frans de Waal, including *Chimpanzee Politics* (New York: Harper and Row,

1982). Vicki Hearne's *Adam's Task* (London, Heinemann, 1986) gives insights from a dog trainer who is also philosophically well informed.

The useful collection *Readings in Animal Cognition*, edited by Marc Bekoff and Dale Jamieson (Cambridge: MIT Press, 1996, 1999), contains a range of articles by philosophers and experts in animal cognition. Tom Regan puts forward arguments that animals can think in *The Case for Animal Rights* (Berkeley: University of California Press, 1984), Chapters 1–2; this view is supported by Dale Jamieson, *Morality's Progress* (Oxford: Oxford University Press, 2002), Chapter 4. Dennett is more sceptical in *Kinds of Mind*, as is Donald Davidson in his article 'Thought and Talk', reprinted in his *Inquiries into Truth and Interpretation* (Oxford: Oxford University Press, 1984). The conversation between Koko and Dr Patterson is reported by The Gorilla Foundation on their website: www.koko.org.

The Call of the Wild, by Jack London (Oxford: Oxford World's Classics, 1998), was first published in 1903.

Chapter 5: Animal Intelligence and Human Minds

The evidence that animals have culture (and can use and make tools) is marshalled by Frans de Waal, *The Ape and the Sushi Master* (London: Penguin, 2002); he also reports the experiments showing that animals can appreciate art and music. Our current understanding of animal intelligence and its limits is described by David Degrazia, *Taking Animals Seriously*, Chapters 6–7, and by Marc Hauser in *Wild Minds*.

Gordon Gallup's 'self-awareness' experiments are reported in his article 'Chimpanzees: Self-recognition', *Science* (1970), pp. 86–7.

Chapter 6: Rights and Moral Status

The difference between rights and moral status is explained in Mary Anne Warren, *Moral Status* (Oxford: Oxford University Press, 1997), Chapter 1; and Regan, *The Case for Animal Rights*, Chapters 6 and 8.

Shylock's great speech appears in Act 3, Scene 1 of Shakespeare's *The Merchant of Venice*.

Chapter 7: The Moral Community

John Rawls's views about justice as a contract are set out in *A Theory of Justice* (Oxford: Oxford University Press, 1972). Peter Carruthers applies contractualist ethical theory to animals in *The Animals Issue*, arguing that animals have no moral status. This view is criticised by Regan in *The Case for Animal Rights*, especially pp. 150–94.

More detailed accounts of animal trials are to be found in E.P. Evans, *The Criminal Prosecution and Capital Punishment of Animals* (London: Heinemann, 1906).

George Orwell's novel *Animal Farm* (London: Penguin, 1994), whose bestial characters represent leading participants in the Russian Revolution, was first published in 1945.

Chapter 8: Pain, Pleasure and the Value of Life

Powerful arguments that any creature that suffers has moral status are given in Chapter 1 of Peter Singer's *Animal Liberation* and Chapter 8 of David Degrazia's *Taking Animals Seriously*.

The view that all living creatures are morally significant is defended by Holmes Rolston III, 'Respect for Life: Counting What Singer Finds of No Account', in D. Jamieson, *Singer and His Critics* (see also Mary Anne Warren, *Moral Status*, Chapters 2–3).

Chapter 9: The Right to Life
A book arguing that great apes are part of our moral community and should have rights, called *The Great Ape Project* and edited by Paola Cavalieri and Peter Singer, was published in 1993 (London: Fourth Estate).

Tom Regan defends animal rights in *The Case for Animal Rights*, Chapters 8–9. Roger Scruton argues that animals do not have rights in *Animal Rights and Wrongs* (London: Demos, 1996), pp. 66–105 (the quoted passage is from p. 67). Peter Singer defends his view of the moral significance of killing humans and animals in *Practical Ethics*, Chapters 4–7.

Jeff McMahan gives very dense and difficult arguments about life and death in humans and animals in *The Ethics of Killing* (Oxford: Oxford University Press, 2003), Chapters 2 and 3.

Chapter 10: All Animals Are Equal …?
Peter Singer discusses the concept of speciesism in Chapter 1 of *Animal Liberation*. Mary Midgley gives a subtle view of discrimination among different humans and between humans and animals in Chapters 7 and 9 of *Animals and Why They Matter* (Athens, GA: University of Georgia Press, 1983).

Anna Sewell's *Black Beauty* (London: Penguin Popular Classics, 1995) was first published in 1877.

Chapter 11: Factory Food
Peter Singer mounts a powerful attack on factory farming in Chapter 3 of *Animal Liberation*. R.M. Hare, another utilitarian, argues for a more moderate view in 'Why I Am Only a Demi-Vegetarian', reprinted in his *Essays on Bioethics* (Oxford: Oxford University Press, 1993), and in *Singer and His Critics*, ed. Dale Jamieson. Tom Regan addresses eating meat in Chapter 9 of *The Case for Animal Rights*.

Roger Scruton defends eating meat (but not factory farms) in his *Animal Rights and Wrongs*, pp. 80–85.

There are some informative fact-sheets on factory farming produced by the Vegetarian Society, available online at www.vegsoc.org, and from the RSPCA at www.rspca.org.uk.

The speech from Old Major appears in the first chapter of Orwell's *Animal Farm*.

Chapter 12: Foxhunting

An invaluable resource on foxhunting is the *Committee of Inquiry into Hunting with Dogs in England and Wales*, popularly known as the *Burns Report* after Lord Burns, the chairman of the committee, which can be found online at www.huntinginquiry.gov.uk.

Roger Scruton defends foxhunting in *Animal Rights and Wrongs*, pp. 87–96. The view that cultural traditions like bull-fighting should be protected is questioned in Paula Casal, 'Is Multi-culturalism Bad for Animals?' *Journal of Political Philosophy*, 2003.

Chapter 13: Science and Suffering

Peter Singer applies utilitarian reasoning to scientific research on animals in Chapter 2 of *Animal Liberation*. A moderate position is defended by Tom Regan and Dale Jamieson in *Morality's Progress*, Chapter 8. Regan later changed his view, and he argues that no experimentation on mammals is warranted in Chapter 9 of *The Case for Animal Rights*.

There are a number of very useful articles on human and animal scientific experimentation collected in the *Blackwell Companion to Bioethics*, ed. Singer and Kuhse (Oxford: Blackwell's, 1998), including Paul McNeill, 'Experimentation on Human Beings', Barbara Orlans, 'History and Ethical Regulation of

Animal Experimentation: An International Perspective', and
Bernard Rollin, 'The Moral Status of Animals and Their Use
as Experimental Subjects'.
Several real-life examples of animal experiments are described in
Barbara Orlans et al., *The Human Use of Animals: Case Studies
in Ethical Choice* (Oxford: Oxford University Press, 1998),
Chapters 2–9.
The animal rights group Animal Aid was a leading figure fighting
against the primate laboratory in Cambridge. There is information about that campaign and about animal experimentation more generally on its website: www.animalaid.org.uk.

Chapter 14: Man's Best Friend?
Aristotle's famous account of friendship is found in Books 8–9 of
Nicomachean Ethics (trans. S. Broadie and C. Rowe, Oxford:
Oxford University Press, 2002). Roger Scruton writes about
companion animals in *Animal Rights and Wrongs*, pp. 69–72.
Vicki Hearne in *Adam's Task* and Raymond Gaita in
The Philosopher's Dog (London: Routledge, 2003) combine
philosophical insight with a love for their dogs. The reunion
of Odysseus and Argos is described in Book 17 of Homer's
Odyssey; and the famously loyal Lassie first appeared in 'Lassie
Come Home', a short story by Eric Knight published in *The
Saturday Evening Post* (1938).

INDEX